How to
Read
Shakespeare

Also by Maurice Charney

Style in "Hamlet"
Shakespeare's Roman Plays
Signet edition of *Timon of Athens*
Bobbs-Merrill edition of *Julius Caesar*

How to Read Shakespeare

by Maurice Charney

McGraw-Hill Book Company

NEW YORK ST. LOUIS SAN FRANCISCO
DUSSELDORF LONDON MEXICO PANAMA
SYDNEY TORONTO

For
Hanna

*Vetulam suam praetulit
immortalitati.*

Library of Congress Catalog Card
Number: 78-169015
First Edition
07-010655-X

Contents

Acknowledgments

This book was begun in the house of Paul Brennan of South Laguna, California, where my neighbors, the Gables, dispensed gracious hospitality and various hand tools. To my colleagues at the Shakespeare Institute of Canada—David Galloway, Terence Hawkes, and Trevor Lennam—I admit to borrowing freely from their witty asides. Bridget Gellert and Ernest Schanzer both read the manuscript with conscientious erudition and a stern eye to faults in style. Ed Doctorow first saw the Platonic image of *How To Read Shakespeare* and had the craft, patience, and good sense to wait for it to appear in the phenomenological world. Under the auspices of its ingenious and witty Associate Director, Fred Main, the Research Council of Rutgers University provided the scholarly leisure in which this book was brought to fruition.

All quotations from Shakespeare are from Peter Alexander's Tudor edition. I owe a profound and unacknowledgeable debt to many books and articles on Shakespeare, from which I have drawn freely as if from the common good.

Introduction

How to Read Shakespeare
Assumes that
Shakespeare's plays
are lively and accessible
to modern readers and spectators.

❨Shakespeare's status as the chief monument of our literature imposes a terrible burden. We remember him as the pillar of our literary education, and we approach his works with a sense of public-spirited devotion. We Shakespearize, but do we read the plays? This book is intended not so much to win new converts to Shakespeare as to persuade intelligent persons to return to the plays with spontaneous, unacademic enthusiasm. Shakespeare has a vigor and intensity of imagination that should immediately be apparent to all readers and spectators.

Drama is a form of public communication, and many of the subtleties and difficulties attributed to Shakespeare are inappropriate to the public character of his plays. It is necessary to reassert that Shakespeare is perspicuous and lucid. In Jan Kott's original and idiosyncratic book, *Shakespeare Our Contemporary*, he insists that Shakespeare must be *our* contemporary in order to be understood by modern audiences. This is a position that historical criticism has always most fiercely opposed, as if the best we could hope for, by patient study, was to become Shakespeare's contemporary.

There are obvious differences in language, thought, and convention between Shakespeare's time and ours, but these difficulties are easily overcome. The notes and commentaries in many editions can help bridge the gap of three and a half centuries. This is merely the homework a reader needs to do in order to bring Shakespeare up to date. Once the reader has learned the basic vocabulary and the fundamentals of Elizabethan staging, he is ready to encounter the plays on their own terms, for this preparatory work is essentially a way of modernizing Shakespeare, or at least translating his works into our own idiom.

Our reading of Shakespeare should try to recover some of the richness and multiplicity of meaning in his plays. There is no point at all in looking for the key that will unlock a certain play—such a key doesn't exist. We should rather be tracking down as many different lines of interest as we can discover. *Hamlet*, for example, is not just a play about Hamlet. Claudius, the secret murderer, is also in it, and Hamlet's mother represents a disturbing sexuality. If there are meditative soliloquies, there are also savage declarations of revenge. Hamlet announces: "Now could I drink hot blood" (3.2.380), and Laertes is ready to cut Hamlet's "throat i' th' church" (4.7.126). The mad Ophelia asserts her presence, singing snatches of bawdy ballads, and the clown-gravediggers jest learnedly on Hamlet's question of mortality: "How long will a man lie i' th' earth ere he rot?" (5.1.158). On the periphery of the action we have the foppish Osric; the ingratiating Rosencrantz and Guildenstern; the frightened soldiers, Marcellus and Bernardo; and the wise and practical friend, Horatio, "A man that Fortune's buffets and rewards/ Hast ta'en with equal thanks" (3.2.65-66). And what about Polonius, that curious medley of comic old man and Machiavellian politician? How can we begin to do justice to the complexity of *Hamlet?* A good reader is one who is not looking for anything in particular, but is sensitive to the experience of what he finds.

In speaking about how to *read* Shakespeare, I recognize frankly that most of us approach his works as readers rather than spectators. It is not often that we can see his plays acted, and performances might distort or fail to realize our own sense of what the plays mean. Even the worst performances, however, are instructive, and it seems to me that there is no conflict of interest between readers and spectators. We begin with the printed text, but in order to appreciate Shakespeare in terms of his own dramatic art, we need to restore a necessary dimension to it. The script of a play is, after all, only the starting point of a production, the score or scenario that must be brought to life by actors in a theater. Nicol Williamson's recent unheroic, passionate, and colloquial Hamlet—the Hamlet of the Midlands, or what we might call the Hamlet of the Middle West—flies in the face of the genteel, Romantic tradition of the black-velvet-collared, lace-shirted, melancholy Dane. And in Peter Brook's production of *A Midsummer Night's Dream*, the fairies float through the air on trapezes, and who are we to say that this levitating device is not beautifully appropriate to the spirit of the play, and that it would not have delighted Shakespeare had he been fortunate enough to think of it?

All this heady talk should not be taken to mean that the rules have been suspended and every man is now free to make up his own Shakespeare. The text imposes restraints, and it is still possible to criticize an interpretation for failing to take account of what the words and the action plainly tell us. But within these limits there is enormous latitude for different views. In some literal sense, Shakespeare is our contemporary because of the opportunities he offers us for creative collaboration. Ben Jonson, who knew and possibly worked with Shakespeare, could carp at his "small Latin and less Greek" and upbraid him for never blotting a line—"would he had blotted a thousand." Yet in what was essential, Jonson could rightly foresee the magnitude of Shakespeare's achievement: "He was not of an age, but for all time!"

Shakespeare's
Career

Who was Gilbert Shakespeare?

《 Contrary to the popular myth that Shakespeare was an obscure, natural genius almost unnoticed in his own time, a good deal is known about his life—more, in fact, than about any other Elizabethan playwright except Ben Jonson. The enthusiastic efforts of researchers have uncovered more than a hundred relevant documents, including deeds to property, entries in parish registers, depositions in law suits, and other legal records.

We even know something about Shakespeare's brother Gilbert, christened on October 13, 1566, and thus more than two years younger than William. From a real estate contract, we learn that on May 1, 1602, Gilbert represented his illustrious brother in the purchase from William and John Combe of "four yard-land within the parish, fields or town of Old Stratford, containing by estimation one hundred and seven acres, with the common of pasture for sheep, horse, kine, or other cattle" for the impressive sum of £320. Gilbert was buried in the parish church of Stratford on February 3, 1612, and was apparently a bachelor.

William's youngest brother was Edmund Shakespeare, who was born in 1580, and who was buried in St. Saviour's Church, Southwark—right in the heart of the London theatrical district of the Bankside—on December 31, 1607. He is listed in the church register as a "player," and he is presumably the same person whose illegitimate son

Edward was buried at the church of St. Giles Cripplegate on August 12 of the same year. William Shakespeare also had a brother Richard, born in 1574, and four sisters: Margaret, Anne, and two Joans, but of all the girls only the second Joan, born in 1569, survived into adulthood. She married William Hart, a hatter, sometime before 1600, and they had three sons, William, Thomas, and Michael. Thus William Shakespeare became an uncle around September 23, 1608, about two weeks after the death of his mother. He had already become a grandfather early in 1608 with the birth of Elizabeth to his daughter Susanna and her husband John Hall.

Shakespeare's family background shows close ties with Stratford and the surrounding area. His mother, Mary Arden, was from Wilmcote, a few miles away, and the attractive, solidly built house in which she lived is still being shown to tourists. John Shakespeare, the father of the dramatist, was from a family that had settled in Snitterfield, a village just outside Stratford, early in the sixteenth century. He was a glover and whittawer (or tanner of white leather), and he also seems to have dealt in farm commodities and real estate. It is unlikely that he was a butcher, although he may have slaughtered some of the animals whose skins he used in his trade. In one of the most literary legends of William Shakespeare's youth, Aubrey, the Restoration biographer, represents him as a histrionic butcher boy, who "exercised his father's trade, but when he killed a calf, he would do it in a high style and make a speech." Aubrey's testimony is piquant but not very reliable, since he was always hunting out private-eye details about famous men, such as the fact that the playwrights Beaumont and Fletcher shared one cloak and one mistress between them and that the philosopher Thomas Hobbes, who loved tennis and singing in bed, was not drunk more than a hundred times in his long life.

John Shakespeare was a substantial citizen of Stratford, who played an important role in local politics. We should not be misled by the fact that he was fined one shilling on

April 29, 1552, for having an unauthorized dunghill on Henley Street—this is surely a sign of prosperity, although his fortunes appear to have declined around 1577. Presumably at his son William's instigation, John Shakespeare was granted by the College of Heralds the right to have his own coat of arms, and the motto "Non Sanz Droict" ("Not Without Right") is associated with this grant. We might look upon this affair as a typical expression of upward mobility by a solid middle-class family. From now on the Shakespeares could write "Gentleman" after their names.

William Shakespeare married a local girl, Anne Hathaway of Shottery, whose substantial cottage is a tourist attraction about an easy mile's walk from the center of Stratford. Shakespeare was eighteen at the time (1582) and Anne twenty-six, and their daughter Susanna was born on May 26, 1583, almost exactly six months later. None of the secrets—if there are any—about Shakespeare's domestic life are known, but these are not the kinds of details that are usually recorded for posterity. There is, for example, nothing particularly derogatory about the "second-best bed" that Shakespeare left Anne in his will, since that may have been the bed they ordinarily slept in, with the best bed reserved for guests. There is no indication that Shakespeare ever lived with his wife and family in London, but we should remember that Stratford is only about a hundred miles away and not a very difficult journey even in the late sixteenth and early seventeenth centuries. There were clearly intervals in the theatrical season when Shakespeare could return home to his family and business interests in Stratford. In London he seems to have lived primarily as a boarder. At the height of his career in 1604, for example, we know that he was dwelling in the house of Christopher Mountjoy, a French Huguenot tire (or headdress) maker on the corner of Silver and Monkwell streets in the parish of St. Giles Cripplegate.

Another material proof of Shakespeare's attachment to his native town is the fact that he made investments in Stratford real estate during his lucrative theatrical career in London. His greatest coup was the purchase in 1597 of a large stone house called New Place right in the center of Stratford. Along with the grant of arms in the previous year, this impressive house and gardens marks Shakespeare's extraordinary success in the business-artistic world of the London theaters. He probably did not begin to live in New Place until about 1610, which seems to indicate his semiretirement from the affairs of the King's Men, the theatrical company with which he was associated. William Shakespeare died in Stratford on April 23, 1616, at almost exactly the age of 52, and he was buried in the chancel of the parish church.

Shakespeare's life has its own independent interest apart from his works. It is only when we try to relate the two that difficulties arise, especially because Shakespeare as a writer is always so impersonal, so objective, and so unrevealing of any particular bias. His characters seem never to be identifiable spokesmen for the author's projected personality, and they draw their imaginative being from their dramatic context rather than from the biographical circumstances of their author. In this perspective, Shakespeare's plays do not reveal anything about Shakespeare the man, and Shakespeare's career in Stratford and London does not offer any special insights into the plays. The many allusions to a Warwickshire setting that critics have found in Shakespeare's works turn out to be much more indebted to literary sources than to topographical reminiscences. Even the homely nature imagery of *Venus and Adonis,* with its "breeding jennet" (= Spanish horse), its "timorous flying hare," and its vivid boar hunt, seems to be derived from classical tradition rather than from personal observation. And the splendid sheep-shearing scene of *The Winter's Tale* is conceived in the artful terms of pastoral rather than those of local Midlands shepherds. Our enthusiastic desire to connect Shakespeare's art and life has tended to falsify both, first by making us try to see Shakespeare the man as a composite of his dramatic characters, and then by imposing on the plays a pattern of fictionalized, biographical expectations.

Shakespeare was the chief play-wright of a repertory company as well as an actor and a theater owner.

⟨ This is an unusual combination of roles, even for an Elizabethan writer, and it demonstrates Shakespeare's thoroughly professional connection with the theater of his time. It is not known precisely when he came to London from Stratford, but by 1592 he is already being denounced by Robert Greene, a popular pamphleteer, for his impertinent success as a playwright. Addressing his fellow "University Wits," Greene writes with allusive scorn of this "upstart crow, beautified with our feathers, that with his tiger's heart wrapped in a player's hide supposes he is as well able to bombast out a blank verse as the best of you, and being an absolute Iohannes factotum, is in his own conceit the only shake-scene in a country." The parody of a recent line from Shakespeare's *Henry VI, Part 3*, clinches the identification: "O tiger's heart wrapp'd in a woman's hide!" (1.4.137).

In 1594, after a period of plague when the theaters were shut, we find Shakespeare as a member of the Lord Chamberlain's Men, which, with the Lord Admiral's Men, were the two leading theatrical companies of the time. Shakespeare remained with this group (called the King's Men at the accession of James I in 1603) during his entire career. In organization and purpose, the Lord Chamberlain's Men were what we would call a repertory company. To avoid prosecution of its players as vagabonds and masterless men, it was under the nominal patronage of the Lord Chamberlain, whose servants the actors were, but the company was actually a self-sufficient corporate entity. It had a central group of "sharers" who owned the stock of the enterprise and directed its activities, including the hiring of journeyman actors and musicians, the apprenticing of boys to play all the female roles, the purchase of costumes and properties, and the acquisition of plays to feed the tremendous demands of repertory.

New plays were presented for runs of not more than a few days, and they were freely interspersed with one-night revivals, which formed the staples of the company. This kind of programing does not demand the mass audience of a Broadway hit. All that is needed for financial success is a faithful following that will keep coming back at least one afternoon a week. The repertory system might explain why the Elizabethan public theaters were built with such huge audience capacities (estimated by theater historians at around 3000), and perhaps also why they were so profitable, especially in the twenty-year period from about 1590 to 1610 that coincides with Shakespeare's own career.

Everything about Shakespeare's plays indicates that he wrote them with the needs and capabilities of the Lord Chamberlain's Men in mind. If there are relatively few women's parts, it is because there may have been only three or four boys capable of playing them, and if there are many songs for the clown, we can be sure that there is a clown in the company capable of singing them. We know that when Will Kempe left the company around 1599 and Robert Armin took his place, the farcical, knockabout clown parts of the earlier plays were replaced by a more lyric and more subtle type of clowning, best seen in the Fool in *Lear*. Over a long period of association, Shakespeare knew the limitations and excellences of his fellow actors, and he wrote parts for them accordingly. It is interesting that all his plays seem to draw on the full resources of the company, about fifteen to twenty actors (assuming that many minor roles would be doubled). Shakespeare has no two- or three-character plays, and he also has no extravaganzas that would bankrupt the Lord Chamberlain's Men with their huge casts.

We know that Shakespeare was himself an actor, although he seems never to have competed with Richard Burbage for the leading roles. His name appears in the cast lists of Ben Jonson's *Every Man in His Humour* (1598) and *Sejanus* (1603), and there is a tradition that he played the old servant Adam in *As You Like It*, the Ghost in *Hamlet*, and perhaps other old men's parts. It is an amusing irony to think of Shakespeare writing the Ghost's cry "Remember me!" when he knew that he himself would utter this exhortation to posterity.

As a sharer in the Lord Chamberlain's Men and the King's Men, Shakespeare had a direct financial stake in the profits of his company. When the Globe was built in 1599, the company then had its own playhouse and no longer needed to pay rents. We know that Shakespeare had a ten percent interest in the Globe, and he also presumably owned part of the private theater in the Blackfriars that the King's Men took over in 1608.

A theater represents a finite number of architectural possibilities, and its physical structure has an important bearing on the kinds of scenes that might best be presented in it. The most striking aspect of the Elizabethan public theater is its thrust or apron stage that extends halfway out into the yard or pit ("orchestra" in modern parlance). We know from the contract for the Fortune theater, which was modeled on the Globe, that it had a stage measuring 43 feet wide and 27½ feet deep, which is a very large acting area by modern notions. The audience standing in the pit surrounded the stage on three sides: these were the cheapest places in the house. An additional charge was made for seats in the galleries that ran in a horseshoe pattern along the back and sides of the theater on at least three levels, and the most expensive seats were in the Lords' Room overlooking the stage at the back, where one could see and be seen at the same time. Perhaps part of the stage itself was also used for seats in full-house performances.

This kind of stage emphasizes close contact with the audience, and certain conventions like soliloquy and aside depend on the actor's being able to come all the way downstage and address the audience directly. In modern theaters built after the Elizabethan model (for example, the Festival Theater in Stratford, Ontario, and the Vivian Beaumont and Forum theaters in Lincoln Center, New York), it is still possible to duplicate this feeling of intimacy with the audience. The actors are standing right in the midst of the audience and not framed in the lighted box of the proscenium-arch theater, into which we may peep by the convention of the missing fourth wall.

There is, of course, no such thing as *the* Elizabethan public theater, but rather individual theaters—the Globe, the Swan, the Fortune, the Rose, the Red Bull, the Curtain, etc.—from which I am trying to draw certain general characteristics. Our most remarkable piece of evidence is a sketch of the Swan theater in about 1595 made by a Dutch visitor, Johannes de Witt, and copied by his friend, Arend van Buchell. Aside from the features already mentioned, there are two massive pillars on stage supporting a roof (or "shadow") that covers less than half of the playing area, and there are two solid, hinged doors at the rear of the stage. Other evidence suggests that staging in the public theaters was meant to be impressive, with rich costumes, elaborate hangings, pillars painted to look like marble, and the tiring-house façade at the back of the stage representing the walls of a city or the fortifications of a castle. The "tiring" or "attiring" house is the area of the dressing rooms, where properties were also stored, and from where the stage machinery was operated. It presumably had at least three levels, as the theater itself did.

The public theaters were unroofed, and they presented their performances in the afternoon by natural light. There were also private theaters in Shakespeare's time that were located indoors, used artificial light, and were much more expensive and elegant than the public theaters. They attracted their audiences by the quality of their music, especially between the acts, and by a more sophisticated and more wittily refined style. These distinctions, however, are not to be taken too literally, since some plays were seen at different times in both public and private theaters. Shakespeare's own commitment seems to have been to the public theaters, although late in his career the King's Men took over the management of the Blackfriars, and this new acquisition may have affected the style of Shakespeare's last romances. These late plays also reflect the influence of masques, which were sumptuous, allegorical presentations, either at court or in a great house, for only one gala performance. In masques, the spectacular costumes, stage effects, music, and dance sometimes make the written text seem a mere scenario.

It was not in the interest of an Elizabethan repertory company to have its plays published, because a rival company might feel free to act them from the printed texts. Manuscripts of plays usually found their way to printers for a number of special reasons. Perhaps the play was no longer of interest to the company, or perhaps the company was being dissolved, or perhaps the sale of the manuscript was needed to raise funds during a period of financial crisis. Some plays were printed from what seem to be stenographic versions of a performance, perhaps pieced out by an actor who took one of the minor roles. Printed plays generally appeared in cheap, hastily composed quarto editions, like our mass-produced paperbacks, which could be read and thrown away by a curious public. The word "quarto" is a printer's term for the format of a book in which the original sheet of paper has been folded twice to produce four leaves (or eight pages).

Nineteen of Shakespeare's plays were printed in quarto editions during his lifetime, some of them hopelessly garbled, and there is no basis at all for believing that he saw any of these editions through the press. It is just possible that Shakespeare as a man of the theater had no interest at all in having his plays published, and, since there was no such thing as an author's copyright in the English Renaissance, he could not have claimed damages for unauthorized editions. We do know that Shakespeare took pains with the publication of the poems *Venus and Adonis* and *The Rape of Lucrece*, proofreading them carefully and embellishing them with dedications. Perhaps printed plays seemed to him grossly inadequate versions of what was actually seen and heard on stage.

Shakespeare's plays were eventually published in a collected edition in 1623, seven years after his death. This is usually called the First Folio, the word "folio" being a printer's term for the format of a book in which the original sheet has been folded only once. Shakespeare's First Folio prints thirty-six plays, of which at least seventeen had never been published before. Thus, when Shake-speare died in 1616, he had no way of knowing that eighteen of his plays (including *Othello*, published in quarto in 1622) would be rescued from oblivion by his friends and fellow sharers of the King's Men, John Heminges and Henry Condell, who prepared the First Folio for the press. The publication of an expensive, collected edition of plays was itself a novelty in the early seventeenth century, and Jonson's *Works*, published in 1616, is perhaps the model for Shakespeare's Folio, although Jonson had been ridiculed by his contemporaries for taking his plays so seriously as literature.

In the light of everything I have said, Shakespeare would certainly find the subject of the present book absurd, since he wrote his plays for theater audiences rather than for readers. Assuming that we can overcome this difficulty by 350 years of indulgence, we may still render Shakespeare a service by trying to read the plays as he wrote them rather than as later editors have rewritten them. It is well to keep in mind that most of our modern editions of Shakespeare are designed for a staging radically different from the Elizabethan public theater for which they were originally intended. The specific locations at the beginning of each scene, for example, have no relevance to Elizabethan staging, and the division into acts and scenes also represents modern practice. It is therefore a distinct pleasure—and one recommended to readers of this book—to look at a Shakespearean play in its early quarto or folio printing. Even without the helpful encumbrances of later editors, readers will be sure to find the play surprisingly intelligible.

The Presented Play: Text and Subtext

We need to pursue both text and subtext simultaneously, so that our perspective is not limited by the verbal form in which the play is set down.

❮ A play is not a novel or a poem. It has a significant nonverbal, presentational aspect that makes demands on us different from our response to words on the printed page. The poetry of the theater is a total effect of all the resources at the playwright's command. In order to recover an aspect of Shakespeare's plays that may be obscured in their printed form, readers should pay particular attention to the stage directions, especially those of the early quartos and the Folio, which are our best guide to Elizabethan theatrical practice. It would also be profitable to study the text for any indications of staging it may contain. By close and imaginative reading, we may invoke the subtext of a performance implied in the words of a play.

Sometimes the stage directions of a Shakespearean play are so carefully developed that we can learn a good deal from them about the meaning of the play. In *Coriolanus,* for example, before any words at all are spoken, *"Enter a company of mutinous Citizens, with staves, clubs, and other weapons."* This violent opening sets the tone for the play, in which the mob exercises a decisive political power. We know at once that something is rotten in the state of Rome. In strong contrast to the beginning, the stage direction of the third scene establishes a domestic atmosphere: "*Enter* VOLUMNIA *and* VIRGILIA, *mother and wife to Marcius; they set them down on two low stools and sew.*" These are the simple joint stools of an Elizabethan household, and the activity of sewing sets this scene apart from the public affairs of the first two scenes. In Elizabethan staging, a few characteristic details are enough to confirm the location.

In the climactic scene of the play (5.3), the stage directions record Volumnia's appeal to her son to have mercy on Rome. Volumnia enters with a family group: Virgilia, Valeria, and young Marcius, all dressed in mourning. Coriolanus kneels to his mother to greet her, but she immediately kneels to him, an act that disturbs her son's sense of decency and propriety. When Coriolanus rises from his seat to leave, he seems to reject all pleas. It is at this point that Volumnia makes her most desperately persuasive assault, which ends with her son's yielding: "*Holds her by the hand, silent*" (5.3.182 s.d.). This is one of the most eloquent stage directions in Shakespeare, and it is especially fitting in a play that contains so much that is hard, cold, and inarticulate. By holding his mother's hand, Coriolanus abandons his godlike isolation and establishes human contact. It is a portentous occasion, and he correctly foresees that it will prove "most mortal to him" (189). The upshot of this scene comes at the very end of the play, when the Volscian conspirators kill Coriolanus. In a final symbolic tableau, his mortal enemy Aufidius "*stands on him*" (5.6.131 s.d.).

Elizabethan staging, as we can recover it from the stage directions, was sometimes very realistic. "*Enter Mariners, wet*" in the storm scene of *The Tempest* (1.1.46 s.d.), and we can be sure that those luckless mariners were doused with water just before they came on. The most spectacular exit in Shakespeare is certainly that of Antigonus in *The Winter's Tale*: "*Exit, pursued by a bear*" (3.3.58 s.d.). This may have been a real bear like Sackerson, who performed at the Paris Garden in Shakespeare's time—Slender tells Mistress Anne Page with bravado: "I have seen Sackerson loose twenty times, and have taken him by the chain" (*The Merry Wives of Windsor* 1.1. 268–69). Or, more likely, the part of the bear was played by an energetic supernumerary, but the effect must have been one of grotesque terror. As the Clown describes it, the bear has only "half din'd on the gentleman; he's at it now" (*The Winter's Tale* 3.3.102–3), and one still presumably hears the roaring of Antigonus off-stage as "the bear tore out his shoulder-bone" (95). At the end of the scene, the Clown will "go see if the bear be gone from the gentleman, and how much he hath eaten" (122–23); and he takes pains to justify the beast's erratic conduct: "They are never curst [= bad-tempered] but when they are hungry" (123–24). Scenes of torture and execution in Shakespeare are equally unsparing of physical details, perhaps nowhere so acutely painful as in the blinding of Gloucester in *King Lear* (3.7).

There is no pattern of realistic staging in *The Winter's Tale* and *The Tempest*, but realistic and symbolic effects exist side by side without any feeling of inconsistency. In *The Tempest*, Ferdinand and Miranda are discovered *"playing at chess"* (5.1.171 s.d.), and this gracious tribute to the powers of reason prepares us for the reconciliations at the end. As a courtly diversion of high-born lovers, the chess game is an emblem of the "marriage of true minds" celebrated in Sonnet CXVI. In *The Winter's Tale* we have the ironic tableau of *"Hermione standing like a statue"* (5.3.20 s.d.), cut in stone by Julio Romano, and with convincing polychromy ("the colour's/ Not dry" 47–48). She is even protected by the typical Renaissance dust curtains, which Paulina must open to reveal the prize of her collection. Is this art or nature? The art-nature theme has been of special importance throughout *The Winter's Tale*, especially in the talk of "gillyvors" or pinks in the sheep-shearing scene, where the innocent Perdita refuses to "put/ The dibble [= hole-making tool for planting] in earth to set one slip of them" (4.4.99–100). Gillyvors are "streak'd" flowers, "Which some call nature's bastards" (83), and their pied coloring associates them with the artifice of painted women. At the end of the play, the staging of Hermione as a statue brings the symbolic theme of art and nature to its culmination.

If we turn now to Shakespeare's text, we find it full of statements and implications about gesture and stage action. At its simplest, the meaning of certain demonstrative pronouns and adverbs is completed only by reference to some actual object, movement, or place on stage. When Polonius informs the King of the love affair between Hamlet and Ophelia, he emphasizes with a gesture the truth of his narration: "Take this from this, if this be otherwise" (2.2.155). The line is incomprehensible unless we can identify the "this's." Most editors follow Lewis Theobald's suggestion of the early eighteenth century that we need a gesture of beheading: "Take this from this" means "Take my head from my shoulders." Gestural words occur everywhere in Shakespeare without any special pattern of distribution. In Falstaff's account of the robbery near Gadshill, he acts out what he is saying: "Thou knowest my old ward: here I lay, and thus I bore my point" (1 *Henry IV* 2.4.187–88). None of these examples is significant in itself, yet as a group they force the reader to translate the demonstrative words into their appropriate gestures.

There are much more important indications of gesture and stage action in Shakespeare's text. Weeping, for example, occurs so frequently that it must have been one of the special skills of an Elizabethan actor. In Lear's recovery from his madness, he recognizes his daughter Cordelia: "Be your tears wet? Yes, faith. I pray weep not" (4.7.71). Lear tests his childlike question by touching Cordelia's cheeks to find out whether her tears are indeed wet. Tears are effeminate, and Enobarbus accuses Antony of making sentimental appeals to his followers:

> What mean you, sir,
> To give them this discomfort? Look, they weep;
> And I, an ass, am onion-ey'd. For shame!
> Transform us not to women.
> (*Antony and Cleopatra* 4.2.33–36)

Laertes, too, does not want to be seen to shed tears, even for his drowned sister:

> Too much of water hast thou, poor Ophelia,
> And therefore I forbid my tears; but yet
> It is our trick; nature her custom holds,
> Let shame say what it will. When these are
>   gone,
> The woman will be out.
>   (*Hamlet* 4.7.186–90)

Thus Laertes weeps against his will, and the intensity of the context suppresses the grotesque wordplay on "water." All of these examples should not suggest that Shakespeare was the Heraclitean, weeping playwright, but only that weeping was an expected form of expression in emotional scenes.

In *Richard II*, which is one of Shakespeare's most gestural plays, the King's return from Ireland begins with happy tears: "I weep for joy/ To stand upon my kingdom once again" (3.2.4–5). Richard then offers a delicately conceited apostrophe to the earth of England: "Dear earth, I do salute thee with my hand" (6). It is difficult to know what gesture is demanded here—the simile of the mother and the child in line 8 suggests a fondling, caressing welcome. There is further insistence on the gesture in the next lines: "So weeping-smiling greet I thee, my earth,/ And do thee favours with my royal hands" (10–11). How, precisely, does Richard execute these "favours" with his "royal hands"? We need to keep in mind that the King is not being filmed on location somewhere along the coast of Wales with "*A castle in view*," as the scene heading in Alexander's edition suggests. He is standing on the bare boards of the Elizabethan stage, and whatever salutes and favors he is offering must be to these boards.

Most of the gestures in Shakespeare have no intrinsic significance, but sometimes the simplest effect has an extraordinary rightness at the moment when it occurs. I am thinking of Charmian's action just after Cleopatra's death by the asps. She shuts her mistress's eyelids:

"Downy windows, close" (5.2.314), then straightens her crown: "Your crown's awry;/ I'll mend it and then play" (316–17). This is a beautiful touch both of devotion to Cleopatra and of the impulse to make her perfect in appearance, like a work of art. When Caesar's Guard comes *"rushing in"* (317 s.d.), Charmian is ready to apply an asp to herself and die "after the high Roman fashion" (4.15.87).

There is an equally affectionate gesture in *Julius Caesar*, when Titinius returns from his scouting mission to find that Cassius has killed himself. Titinius removes his own "wreath of victory" (5.3.82) so that he may adorn Cassius with it:

> But hold thee, take this garland on thy brow;
> Thy Brutus bid me give it thee, and I
> Will do his bidding.
>
> (5.3.85–87)

The wreath memorializes an heroic death, but it is also the conventional Roman symbol of triumph. Like Charmian and Cleopatra, Titinius proves his devotion to Cassius by acting "a Roman's part" (89); he kills himself with the same bloody sword that Cassius used.

Every play of Shakespeare has stage properties that define its distinctive quality.

❬ In his *Short View of Tragedy* (1692), Thomas Rymer may have had a shrewd point when he said that *Othello* was "a warning to all good wives that they look well to their linen." By putting so much stress on Desdemona's lost handkerchief, Othello chooses to interpret his wife's fidelity in Rymer's domestic terms. It is the "ocular proof" he has been demanding with so much frenzied anticipation, as the psychologist Iago keenly understands:

Trifles light as air
Are to the jealous confirmations strong
As proofs of holy writ . . . .
(3.3.326–28)

That something so trivial as a handkerchief can have such
a catastrophic effect is a measure of Othello's own tragic
blindness.

In *Romeo and Juliet*, we think immediately of the
potent drugs by which Romeo kills himself and by which
Juliet is cast into a deathlike trance. When we first meet
Friar Lawrence, the voice of reason and good sense in the
play, he is gathering "baleful weeds and precious-juiced
flowers" (2.3.8). His botany is emblematic:

Within the infant rind of this weak flower
Poison hath residence, and medicine power;
For this, being smelt, with that part cheers
   each part;
Being tasted, slays all senses with the heart.
Two such opposed kings encamp them still
In man as well as herbs—grace and rude will;
And where the worser is predominant,
Full soon the canker death eats up that
   plant.
(2.3.23–30)

The Friar uses his stage properties to demonstrate the
moral forces that lie at the heart of the tragedy.

It may be profitable, as an experiment, to consider
certain plays of Shakespeare chiefly in terms of their properties. In *The Comedy of Errors*, for example, the farcical
action animates the properties and mechanizes the persons.
Properties are mistaken as readily as persons, and, once
set in motion, the properties have a life of their own;
they bounce off the persons without any feeling of intrinsic attachment. We need to wait for the end of the play
until the whole loot is distributed to its rightful owners,
and properties and persons are securely joined to each
other. The complications begin in Act I, scene ii, when
the First Merchant gives Antipholus of Syracuse the

money he has been keeping for him: a bag of gold containing a thousand marks, which Antipholus entrusts to his servant Dromio. The entrance of Dromio of Ephesus disturbs the tranquillity of Antipholus, since the wrong servant knows of no money, but earnestly importunes his supposed master to come home to dinner. And so it goes. When Angelo the goldsmith presents Antipholus of Syracuse with the gold chain—the "carcanet" (3.1.4)—he ordered for his wife, the wrong Antipholus finds it difficult to refuse such unlooked-for bounty:

> I see a man here needs not live by shifts,
> When in the streets he meets such golden
>   gifts.
>
> (3.2.180–81)

Meanwhile, the irate Antipholus of Ephesus sends his servant Dromio to buy a "rope's end" (4.1.16), with which he plans to beat his wife and her confederates. When, however, he is arrested for debt, he gives the wrong Dromio the key to his desk in order to obtain a purse of ducats from his wife as bail. Luciana, the sister-in-law, presents Dromio with the purse, which he promptly hands over to Antipholus of Syracuse, who is conspicuously sporting the gold chain. As the confusion of properties mounts, no one at all seems concerned about questions of identity. Suddenly, a Courtezan appears claiming a diamond ring of Antipholus, which he supposedly took from her at dinner with the promise to give her a gold chain. Later, we see Antipholus of Ephesus with that very diamond on his finger. In the midst of all these tumultuous errors, *"Enter* DROMIO *of Ephesus, with a rope's-end"* (4.4.7 s.d.). This is a property we have forgotten, and Antipholus of Ephesus is dumbfounded by the sudden, skyrocketing inflation in his native city: "Five hundred ducats, villain, for a rope?" (13). In moments of crisis, both Antipholuses resort to the traditional expedient of farce: beating their servants, whichever Dromio happens to be handy.

In *Titus Andronicus*, which is Shakespeare's first tragedy, he delights in displaying his powers of histrionic invention, especially in spectacular scenes and properties. There is a determined effort to make the villainy of Aaron the Moor seem creative and original. With sardonic glee, Aaron persuades Titus to cut off his left hand in order to save the lives of his two sons. Not only does Titus believe him, but he also asks Aaron to do the cutting. Suddenly, Titus sees the futility of his sacrifice: *"Enter a Messenger, with two heads and a hand"* (3.1.234 s.d.). The decapitated head, held by the hair, was a familiar Elizabethan property, and it could be artfully made up to resemble any character. In *Cymbeline*, for example, Guiderius enters *"with Cloten's head"* (4.2.113 s.d.). At the end of Act III, scene i, of *Titus Andronicus*, Titus disposes of the properties with a grotesque practicality:

> Come, brother, take a head,
> And in this hand the other will I bear.
> And, Lavinia, thou shalt be employ'd in this;
> Bear thou my hand, sweet wench, between
>   thy teeth.
>
> (3.1.280–83)

There is no sentimental squeamishness in this scene, which is either funny or hideous.

Although Lavinia has had her tongue cut out and her hands chopped off, she is able to disclose that she has also been raped—and by whom—with extraordinary ingenuity. She manages to get hold of her little nephew's copy of Ovid's *Metamorphoses*, whose pages she turns to the "tragic tale of Philomel" (4.1.48). Then, with even more admirable resourcefulness, her uncle Marcus *"writes his name with his staff, and guides it with feet and mouth"* (69 s.d.), setting an example for Lavinia: *"She takes the staff in her mouth and guides it with her stumps, and writes"* (77 s.d.). The young Shakespeare must have been proud of himself for devising such a highly wrought stage action, with its gracious tribute to Ovid, his earliest literary master.

*Costumes are an important
means of characterization, with
changes in costume to mark
changes in role.*

❨ The frantic brilliance of *Titus Andronicus* owes as
much to costumes as to properties. Costumes are, in fact,
a kind of personal property that helps to define character,
or at least to make certain points about character in an
immediate, external way. Titus, for example, uses costume
and properties together when he enters *"like a cook, plac-
ing the dishes"* (5.3.25 s.d.) for the banquet that concludes the play. This is the moment he has been waiting
for, and he displays his fatal *pièce de résistance* with all
the satisfaction of a Cordon Bleu chef:

> Why, there they [= the two sons of Tam-
>   ora] are, both baked in this pie,
> Whereof their mother daintily hath fed,
> Eating the flesh that she herself hath bred.
>   (5.3.60–62)

Readers of Shakespeare need to take account of this
strong visual emphasis. We know that costumes were the
single largest expense of an Elizabethan production, and
in an age when the symbolism of dress was much more
specific than it is today, characters in plays would be
judged by the strict standards of daily life. When Cleopatra
says, "Show me, my women, like a queen" (5.2.226), the
"best attires" of the stage wardrobe must compete with
the real queens and royal personages the audience has
seen. The afternoon performance and the nearness of the
spectators to the stage would also encourage a high degree
of fidelity in the costumes.

Elizabethan clothes were much closer to what we would
call uniforms. Each trade and each social class had its
characteristic costume, and there were even sumptuary
ordinances that forbade, under penalty of law, the usurpa-
tion of a style to which a person was not entitled. Costume offers an immediate insight into a character's pro-

fession, trade, social status, affiliation, nationality, and general standing in the world. The servants of a great house wore the livery of that house, with its appropriate heraldic devices, which makes it easy to distinguish Capulets from Montagues in *Romeo and Juliet*. One function of theatrical costume, then, is to define with unmistakable clarity different groups—especially hostile groups—on stage.

Readers of Shakespeare are called upon to supply some of the immediate connotations of costume that would be apparent to an Elizabethan audience. How are we to interpret: *"Enter* ARIEL, *invisible"* (*The Tempest* 2.1.175 s.d.)? Ariel is presumably wearing a garment like the one described in the accounts of Philip Henslowe, the theatrical entrepreneur, for April 3, 1598: "Bowght a robe for to goo invisibell." Prospero, too, appears *"invisible"* *"on the top"* of the theater (3.3.17 s.d.), and in A *Midsummer Night's Dream*, Puck needs to be invisible to carry out the commands of Oberon.

Ghosts in Shakespeare probably all dressed in a recognizably "ghostly" style, so that we would recognize them at once. The eleven spirits that appear in series to Richard III and to Henry, Earl of Richmond, on the night before the battle at Bosworth Field, must have seemed sufficiently wraithlike to make the right impression. Perhaps they were all made up in white-face; clothed in sheets, flowing robes, or silvered-leather armor; and trained to speak in a slow, high-pitched, portentous tone. Ghosts were also supposed to smell of sulphur (from their underworld associations) and to cause a candle to burn blue or to sputter.

Fancy dress, or what the Elizabethans called "bravery," seems always to have pejorative connotations in Shakespeare. Between two armies, the better dressed usually loses. This is a point much emphasized in the battle of Agincourt in *Henry* V. The French are fresh and gallantly costumed; the English war-weary and battle-stained. King Henry speaks proudly of this distinction in the parley before the battle:

> We are but warriors for the working-day;
> Our gayness and our gilt are all besmirch'd
> With rainy marching in the painful field;
> There's not a piece of feather in our host—
> Good argument, I hope, we will not fly—
> And time hath worn us into slovenry.
> But, by the mass, our hearts are in the
>   trim . . . .

$$(4.3.109-15)$$

The French plumes that Henry abjures are a significant visual detail. In *Julius Caesar*, Shakespeare follows Plutarch in giving the army of the conspirators fastidious battle array. As Antony tells us, they

> come down
> With fearful bravery, thinking by this face
> To fasten in our thoughts that they have
>   courage;
> But 'tis not so.

$$(5.1.9-12)$$

The symbolism of costume is often used in its most traditional way by Shakespeare to represent a false appearance, so that there is something immediately suspect about armies that dress up.

The theatricality of his costume exposes Malvolio to ridicule in *Twelfth Night*. His self-love is manifested in an insatiable vanity about his clothes, which lays the basis for the plot against him. Just before he finds Maria's letter, he imagines himself married to Olivia and lording it over her household, "Calling my officers about me, in my branch'd velvet gown" (2.5.44–45)—he has a precise eye for details of dress and interior furnishings. Maria's feigned letter from Olivia appeals to Malvolio's interest in fashion: "Remember who commended thy yellow stockings, and wish'd to see thee ever cross-garter'd. I say, remember.'" (136–37). Malvolio vows to follow all the prescriptions in the letter, when the truth of the matter is that yellow is a color Olivia "abhors, and cross-garter'd, a fashion she detests" (180–81). These specifications must have been strongly evocative for an Elizabethan audience, especially the old-fashioned style of cross-gartering both above and below the knee. Malvolio's aberrations in dress are taken as a sign of madness, and, in an age without alienists, Elizabethan madness manifests itself by conventional tokens, such as disheveled and irrational clothes, or, for the ladies, letting one's hair down—in *Troilus and Cressida*, the prophetess Cassandra enters *"raving"* and *"with her hair about her ears"* (2.2.100 s.d.).

In tragedy, the verbal imagery of clothing works together with stage costume to emphasize deceitful appearances. As in popular iconography, truth is naked, while "Robes and furr'd gowns hide all" (*King Lear* 4.6.165). From the sumptuous royal figure of the first scene, Lear moves toward some literal understanding of "Poor naked wretches" (3.4.28) and the "poor, bare, forked animal" represented by "unaccommodated man." This radical insight is translated into an uncontrollable impulse to get rid of his tainted clothes: "Off, off, you lendings! Come, unbutton here" (106-8).

In *Macbeth*, too, there is an interplay between the actual costumes and the powerful imagery of clothes. We are made painfully aware that Macbeth's new clothes do not fit him properly, so that his honors "Hang loose about him, like a giant's robe/ Upon a dwarfish thief" (5.2.21–22). Like Coriolanus in the gown of humility begging the votes of the plebeians, Macbeth is uncomfortable in the ceremonial garments that are a sign of his new status: "The Thane of Cawdor lives; why do you dress me/ In borrowed robes?" (1.3.108–9). This uneasy, childlike feeling that his clothes are not his own persists throughout the play and helps to intensify Macbeth's tragic anxieties.

Off-stage sounds comment on the action and broaden our perspective of what is happening on stage.

❡ Sound effects play an important role in the nonverbal presented play that lies behind our reading of Shakespeare.

In *Julius Caesar,* for example, the flourishes and shouts of the Roman populace that we hear applauding Caesar in the market place show a significant aspect of Caesar's political ambition. At least that is how Cassius interprets these sounds in his attempt to win Brutus to the conspiracy. The comments of Brutus indicate how powerfully affected he is by what he hears:

> What means this shouting? I do fear the
>   people
> Choose Caesar for their king.
>
> (1.2.79–80)

> Another general shout!
> I do believe that these applauses are
> For some new honours that are heap'd on
>   Caesar.
>
> (1.2.132–34)

The wily Cassius knows how to manipulate Brutus's fears and to suggest meanings that Brutus only partially apprehends.

Shakespearean tempests show nature as the moral context for human events. Through its association with Jupiter, thunder expresses the displeasure of the gods with something amiss on earth. Lear, shut out on the heath by Regan and Goneril, discovers symbolic meanings in the wild and tempestuous night:

> Let the great gods,
> That keep this dreadful pudder o'er our
>   heads,
> Find out their enemies now. Tremble, thou
>   wretch,
> That hast within thee undivulged crimes
> Unwhipp'd of justice.
>
> (3.2.49–53)

The "dreadful pudder" of the gods is a sign of imminent justice, and Lear seems to be thinking specifically of the Day of Doom, when the destruction of the world will be followed by the Last Judgment:

> Blow, winds, and crack your cheeks; rage,
>   blow.

> You cataracts and hurricanoes, spout
> Till you have drench'd our steeples, drown'd
>   the cocks.
> You sulph'rous and thought-executing fires,
> Vaunt-couriers of oak-cleaving thunderbolts,
> Singe my white head. And thou, all-shaking
>   thunder,
> Strike flat the thick rotundity o' th' world;
> Crack nature's moulds, all germens spill at
>   once,
> That makes ingrateful man.
>   (3.2.1–9)

The sound effects of this storm—the thunder, lightning, and wind—are not meant to be convincing in themselves, but they keep us aware of a dimension of the play above and beyond the human participants. The external tempest is paralleled by the tempest in Lear's mind; madness is the equivalent of the disorder in nature.

Another symbolic possibility for thunder is its connection with the diabolic forces, as in *Macbeth*. The three witches always appear "In thunder, lightning, or in rain" (1.1.2), and they are associated with the baleful powers both of bad weather and of spiritual destruction:

> Fair is foul, and foul is fair:
> Hover through the fog and filthy air.
>   (1.1.10–11)

They promise that the master of the *Tiger*, whose wife has offended them, shall be "tempest-tost" (1.3.25), and in Act IV, scene i, thunder precedes the showing of the apparitions.

Sound effects were also used to represent the passage of time, which is difficult to do persuasively in the outdoor, afternoon performance of the Elizabethan public theater. In the enclosed, private theaters, the dimming of candles could effectively indicate night—not so effectively, perhaps, as our modern rheostats, yet still well enough for a conventional purpose. In the public theater, the tolling of a bell imitated the church bells that marked the hour. At the beginning of *Hamlet*, for example, there is an impressive ringing of midnight, the time of the changing of the guard at Elsinore. " 'Tis now struck twelve," says Bernardo, "get thee to bed, Francisco" (1.1.7). Toward the end of the scene, *The cock crows* (138 s.d.), and the approach of daylight forces the Ghost to return to its confine.

In *Romeo and Juliet,* the sounds the lovers hear on their wedding night seem to be purely a matter of poetic description. Juliet initiates the debate between the nightingale and the lark:

> Wilt thou be gone? It is not yet near day;
> It was the nightingale, and not the lark,
> That pierc'd the fearful hollow of thine ear;
> Nightly she sings on yond pomegranate tree.
> Believe me, love, it was the nightingale.
> (3.5.1–5)

Even though it is unlikely that these birds were imitated off-stage, as the cock in *Hamlet* certainly was, they still illustrate how time can be represented by characteristic sounds.

Dramatic
Conventions

Dramatic conventions offer a
convenient shorthand
that frees the playwright from
laborious explanations.

⟨ All communication is highly conventional. We recognize a significant gesture or a meaningful intonation because we immediately understand the complex assumptions on which that gesture or intonation is based. Convention allows for a great deal of condensation in our language. We don't need to begin at the beginning, so that by common consent we are free to develop implications without ever establishing their basis. In literature, convention always depends upon what Coleridge called "that willing suspension of disbelief for the moment, which constitutes poetic faith." In other words, both writer and reader agree to accept the fiction as imaginative truth. The theater is particularly dependent upon conventions, because it is a public and oral form that needs to make its points swiftly and unambiguously. Even the most realistic modern stage-set still relies on the convention of the fourth wall, since the audience could not see the drawing room with solid sofas, real lamps, and authentic drinks (with ice cubes) unless the wall facing the spectators had been removed.

Elizabethan theatrical conventions are similar in principle to those in the modern theater. It is evident that conventions generally develop in relation to methods of staging, and especially to the limitations of those methods. Before the use of electricity, for example, there were many different ways of representing night. In the afternoon performance of the Elizabethan public theater, torches were brought on stage, or candles were lit, or, most frequently, a descriptive passage was introduced to set the scene. Some of Shakespeare's most memorable poetry is devoted to these atmospheric descriptions, as in the wooing of Romeo and Juliet:

> Thou knowest the mask of night is on my
>   face,
> Else would a maiden blush bepaint my
>   cheek
> For that which thou hast heard me speak
>   to-night.
>
> (2.2.85–87)

> O blessed, blessed night! I am afeard,
> Being in night, all this is but a dream,
> Too flattering-sweet to be substantial.
>
> (2.2.139–41)

We know that it is night in *Romeo and Juliet* because the characters keep insisting on it, and it is disquieting to think how Shakespeare might have written this love scene if the splendors of modern stage lighting had been at his disposal. In order to function, conventions need a tacit agreement between playwright and audience about what to expect. Once we know what the rules are, it is not difficult for us to suspend our disbelief, because we are trained as an audience to respond in the right way.

One of the most striking conventions of the Elizabethan theater was that boy actors played all the female roles. Boys were apprenticed to senior members of the company in order to be taught the "mystery" or profession of acting, and they must have been successful impersonators, because when actresses began to appear in the Restoration, some nostalgic old-timers complained that the boys were more convincing. Shakespeare is constantly reminding us that his women are being played by boys. At a crucial moment in *Antony and Cleopatra*, when Cleopatra is trying to decide whether to yield to Caesar or to kill herself, she imagines her capitulation in completely theatrical terms:

> the quick comedians
> Extemporally will stage us, and present
> Our Alexandrian revels; Antony
> Shall be brought drunken forth, and I shall
>   see
> Some squeaking Cleopatra boy my greatness
> I' th' posture of a whore.
>
> (5.2.215–20)

The squeaking of a cracked voice is the chief liability of a boy approaching adolescence, and the "in-joke" helps to relieve tensions.

One effect of the boy actor convention is that Shakespeare conceives his female roles differently from those in modern plays. Much more is made to depend on language than on external charms, and scenes of physical passion are more or less excluded. It is not out of hardness of heart that Shakespeare restricts his embraces, but because of the practical necessities of the staging. Modern editors seem determined to make up for this tactile poverty by supplying in square brackets all sorts of additional loving gestures that would have been embarrassing to an Elizabethan audience. At the beginning of *Antony and Cleopatra*, for example, Antony tells Cleopatra:

> Let Rome in Tiber melt, and the wide arch
> Of the rang'd empire fall! Here is my space.
> Kingdoms are clay; our dungy earth alike
> Feeds beast as man. The nobleness of life
> Is to do thus . . . .
>
> (1.1.33–37)

Most editors interpret "thus" in the last line as "*embracing*," but Antony is more likely to mean that the nobleness of life is to do as he does: to ignore the messengers and let Rome go to the devil. In the logic of Elizabethan staging, Antony would not be eager at this point to embrace his preadolescent co-star.

Because dramatists work within the limits of their craft, there are no "dumb blondes" in Shakespeare—his women appeal to us chiefly by their wit. They tend to be brighter, livelier, more imperturbable, and more malicious than their male counterparts. In the "merry war" between Beatrice and Benedick in *Much Ado About Nothing*, Beatrice clearly has the upper hand. The war between the sexes is multiplied fourfold in *Love's Labour's Lost*, where the women show up the absurdities of the men, both as monastics and as Muscovites, and even set them penances at the end. This dominance of women is particularly strong in Shakespeare's early comedies, but the principle still holds true for *Romeo and Juliet*, in which Juliet is more charming and inventive than the romantic Romeo. As a general rule, Shakespeare's women have a lyric sensitivity that would be inappropriate for his men. They feel more strongly, and, in the extremes of passion, are capable of wild poetic license in mad scenes such as those of Ophelia, the Jailer's Daughter (in *The Two Noble Kinsmen*), and Lady Macbeth.

If Shakespeare wrote his plays with the capabilities of his company in mind, sometimes a special characteristic of that company seems to show through the plays. In *A Midsummer Night's Dream*, for example, Helena calls the distraught Hermia "puppet," and Hermia's stinging reply dwells on that point:

> 'Puppet!' why so? Ay, that way goes
> the game.
> Now I perceive that she hath made
> compare
> Between our statures; she hath urg'd
> her height;
> And with her personage, her tall personage,
> Her height, forsooth, hath prevail'd with
> him [=Lysander].
> And are you grown so high in his esteem
> Because I am so dwarfish and so low?
> How low am I, thou painted maypole?
> Speak.

> How low am I? I am not yet so low
> But that my nails can reach unto thine eyes.
> (3.2.289–98)

Although Helena has the advantage in height, she is genuinely terrified by the fierce Hermia:

> Your hands than mine are quicker for a fray;
> My legs are longer though, to run away.
> (3.2.342–43)

The boy actors who played these parts were undoubtedly such an odd pair that Shakespeare felt the need to call attention to them in his comedies of this period. Rosalind in *As You Like It* describes herself as "more than common tall" (1.3.111) and therefore better able to disguise as a man than the shorter Celia. The mild and dulcet Hero in *Much Ado About Nothing* is "Leonato's short daughter" (1.1.184) whereas the witty and satirical Beatrice is presumably the tall girl. This pairing probably also applies to *The Taming of the Shrew*, where, as in *A Midsummer Night's Dream*, it may be reversed for farcical effect, so that Katherine may be the "wild-cat" (1.2.193) who terrifies her tall but placid sister, Bianca. The only reasonable conclusion from these examples is that Shakespeare is exploiting the resources of his company—not only exploiting them, but also making capital out of what might seem to be a serious liability.

A dramatic convention is an arbitrary agreement between playwright and audience that will work to their mutual benefit. On the Elizabethan stage the convention of the impenetrability of disguise frees the playwright from the need to make disguise convincing—all disguise is good disguise; a mere change of name or costume and a bit of false beard creates a different person. No thorough alteration is necessary or even desirable, because the character may want to shift back quickly to his original role. The most common disguise is for a young maiden in love to become a page, so that she can enter the service of her beloved lord. In *Twelfth Night*, Viola serves Duke Orsino as Caesario, who is not quite the figure Shakespeare originally intended—in Viola's first scene she asks the Captain to present her to the Duke "as an eunuch" (1.2.56). Rosalind in *As You Like It* is metamorphosed into Ganymede, and thereby woos Orlando with greater freedom, and Julia in *The Two Gentlemen of Verona* becomes Sebastian in order to pursue her reluctant lover, Proteus. None of these changes goes beyond a few external features, yet they are wondrously effective. By catching their men off-guard, the girls always win the love game, and no one ever considers their disguise a form of duplicity.

The transvestism of Shakespeare's comedies has the pleasant air of a costume party, in which the boy actors are sometimes allowed to play boys, with all the affected irony this involves. In *The Two Gentlemen of Verona*, the conversation of Julia with her waiting woman develops some of the sexual implications of male dress:

> *Lucetta.* You must needs have them [= the
>   breeches] with a codpiece, madam.
> *Julia.* Out, out, Lucetta, that will be ill-
>   favour'd.
> *Lucetta.* A round hose, madam, now's not
>   worth a pin,
>   Unless you have a codpiece to stick
>   pins on.
>   (2.7.53–56)

The codpiece, or padded flap in front of a man's breeches, is an amusingly self-conscious detail for the audience. Costumed as a man, Rosalind in *As You Like It* promises, with "A gallant curtle-axe upon my thigh,/ A boar spear in my hand," to show "a swashing and a martial outside" (1.3.113–14, 116)—a figure like the intrepid Adonis in the poem *Venus and Adonis*. Disguise raised no problems for Shakespeare and the Elizabethan dramatists because the plays were rhetorical, artful, and formal, and they made no attempt to conceal the workings of their sometimes outlandish plots. By making the disguise convention so simple, Shakespeare seems to be asserting that dramatic characters are not such fixed and immutable "personalities" as we seem to think.

*The conventions of soliloquy
and aside allow characters to
address the audience directly,
outside the dialogue form.*

❧ The Elizabethan soliloquy and aside are closely related in purpose. In soliloquy, the speaker is alone on stage and speaks to the audience; in aside, the speaker is never alone, but makes brief comments, often epigrammatic, that are not part of the spoken dialogue. There are also some soliloquies in which the speaker is not actually alone on stage, and some asides that are spoken "apart" to another character, yet neither the soliloquy nor the aside can be overheard, even by a secretly placed eavesdropper. Theatrical convention establishes a convenient barrier for soliloquies and asides, so that a character has undisturbed license to speak his mind. This Elizabethan freedom from the bondage of dialogue has attracted modern playwrights, especially Eugene O'Neill, who tried to revive soliloquy and aside as the inner voice of conscience and guilt.

The design of Shakespeare's apron stage helped to give soliloquy and aside their maximum effectiveness. On this large stage that extended into the middle of the "pit," a character could come all the way downstage to address the audience in a familiar, confidential tone. The stage situation of soliloquies and asides put the speaker right in the midst of the audience, who surrounded the acting area on three sides. In this context, direct addresses to the audience seem perfectly reasonable, and even though the standing audience in the "pit" had the cheapest places in the house, they would still, by the mere rights of propinquity, remain the arbiters of the play. Elizabethan actors must have known that their success or failure depended upon the "groundlings," and they took pains to win them over. The feeling is like that of our theater in the round or cabaret or burlesque, whose runways are a frank acknowledgment of audience contact.

The soliloquy in Shakespeare and Elizabethan drama is frequently the means by which the villain informs the audience how clever he is and how stupid everyone else is, and how easy it will therefore be for him to triumph over his decent but credulous adversaries. This soliloquy manifesto of the villain usually occurs at the end of his first scene, although it can also come at the beginning, as in the vaunting soliloquy of Richard, Duke of Gloucester, that opens *Richard III*. His first words celebrate the peace of England assured by the House of York:

> Now is the winter of our discontent
> Made glorious summer by this sun of York;
> And all the clouds that lour'd upon our
>   house
> In the deep bosom of the ocean buried.
>   (1.1.1–4)

The tranquillity of this moment is, of course, deceptive, and Richard dwells with sardonic glee on his own monstrous inappropriateness for an heroic age:

> I—that am curtail'd of this fair proportion,
> Cheated of feature by dissembling nature,
> Deform'd, unfinish'd, sent before my time
> Into this breathing world scarce half made
>   up,
> And that so lamely and unfashionable
> That dogs bark at me as I halt by them . . . .
>   (1.1.18–23)

By a twist in logic, he makes his villainy spring from his deformity:

> And therefore, since I cannot prove a lover
> To entertain these fair well-spoken days,
> I am determined to prove a villain
> And hate the idle pleasures of these days.
>   (1.1.28–31)

He then reveals to us his plot to set his brothers Clarence and Edward in deadly hate against each other. He makes no attempt at all to mitigate his own corruption. The plot, in fact, depends upon King Edward's being "as true and just/ As I am subtle, false, and treacherous." Richard's soliloquy is neither profound nor poetic, but its boldness gives the illusion of true confession from the very lips of the villain.

In *Othello*, we have to wait until the action is well under way for Iago's soliloquy, which concludes the first act. Like Richard, Iago seems to be confessing all to the audience, and, by letting them in on his secret, he hopes to win their sympathy and appreciation. Both villains speak with disarming frankness, common sense, and manly forthrightness. Iago is especially concerned lest we mistake Roderigo for his friend:

> Thus do I ever make my fool my purse;
> For I mine own gain'd knowledge should
> profane
> If I would time expend with such a snipe
> But for my sport and profit.
>
> (1.3.377–80)

He is excessively proud of his art, his "gain'd knowledge," which he feels he will "profane"—this is a strong word—unless it produce "sport and profit," a characteristically pragmatic combination.

From this statement of principle, or at least of tactics, Iago moves into his plot against Othello. The soliloquy has an attractively colloquial quality, as if Iago were making it all up as he goes along: "Let me see now" (386), "How, how? Let's see" (388), completed by "I ha't—it is engender'd" (397). Psychologically, this is not very subtle, but it serves to show us Iago in action. Everything is made to depend on Othello's uprightness and candor, public virtues that Iago scorns:

> The Moor is of a free and open nature
> That thinks men honest that but seem to
> be so;
> And will as tenderly be led by th' nose
> As asses are.
>
> (1.3.393–96)

There is something frightening in the villain's insolent contempt for his victim.

The importance of soliloquy in Shakespearean drama has been much exaggerated by Romantic critics, who considered it the soul of the play—an intense and passionate moment when a character, relieved of the trivialities of conversation, may finally utter poetic truths. There are few soliloquies of this apocalyptic sort in Shakespeare. After all, the soliloquizer is not speaking only to himself but also to the audience, which does not merely overhear by chance what he says, but participates as directly in his speech—perhaps more so—as in ordinary dialogue. Most soliloquies in Shakespeare have an expository function. They communicate information to the audience, or establish attitudes, or reveal the truth that lies hidden behind appearances. In other words, they are not simply expressive or philosophical (although they are sometimes that, too), but play a significant role in the development of the dramatic action.

This is true even of the soliloquies of Hamlet, a character central to the Romantic theory of creative self-expression. His soliloquies are not detachable displays of eloquence, but are closely related to their theatrical context. In his first soliloquy, for example, we are made to feel that this is the only form of expression available to him in the hostile court of Claudius's Denmark. Of the first 128 lines of Act I, scene ii, Hamlet speaks only 15 lines, but when he is left alone on stage, he suddenly explodes into a series of wild exclamations. He begins with a desire for annihilation and anonymity like Richard II's "mockery king of snow" (4.1.260):

> O, that this too too solid flesh would melt,
> Thaw, and resolve itself into a dew!
> (1.2.129–30)

The Christian prohibition against suicide forces Hamlet to endure with loathing the "weary, stale, flat, and unprofitable . . . uses of this world" (133–34). We cannot imagine this sort of discourse in dialogue, not even with the good Horatio—the use of soliloquy obviates the wooden convention of the confidant. Hamlet speaks directly to the audience without any intermediary, and he reveals an outraged grief for his dead father quite unlike the smooth platitudes of Claudius and Gertrude.

Soliloquy encourages a much freer and more frenzied expression than is possible in dialogue:

> and yet, within a month—
> Let me not think on't. Frailty, thy name is
> woman!—
> A little month, or ere those shoes were old
> With which she followed my poor father's
> body,
> Like Niobe, all tears—why she, even she—
> O God! a beast that wants discourse of
> reason
> Would have mourn'd longer—married with
> my uncle,
> My father's brother . . . .
>
> (1.2.145–52)

The broken syntax provides histrionic emphasis on a truth about his mother Hamlet finds difficult to accept. There is incantatory repetition of that profane month since his father's death, and we could say in general that the soliloquy is full of emotional self-indulgence. When Hamlet sees Horatio, Marcellus, and Bernardo approaching, he knows that he must abandon the soliloquy form: "But break, my heart, for I must hold my tongue" (159).

The asides in Shakespeare help to control the dramatic irony.

⟨ By reminding us of the multiple aspects of a scene, asides function as a truth-telling device. In *Julius Caesar*, for example, when the conspirators persuade Caesar to go to the senate, we know that he is going to his doom, so that his loving courtesy is ironically misdirected. To Trebonius he says with familiarity:

> What, Trebonius!
> I have an hour's talk in store for you.
> Remember that you call on me to-day;
> Be near me, that I may remember you.
>
> (2.2.120–23)

Trebonius answers perfunctorily, "Caesar, I will," but in his aside he plays viciously on Caesar's word: "And so near will I be,/ That your best friends shall wish I had been further" (124–25).

Caesar continues with gracious hospitality:

> Good friends, go in and taste some wine with
> me;
> And we, like friends, will straightway go
> together.
>
> (2.2.126–27)

Brutus's aside also ironically plays on Caesar's word:

> That every like is not the same, O Caesar,
> The heart of Brutus earns to think upon!
> (2.2.128–29)

"Earns" is a strong word for grieves, and Brutus's aside expresses the tragic deception of this scene. The conspiracy forces Brutus into a false position. He, too, is acting "like" Caesar's friend only in order to entrap him; he is betraying his honesty by drinking wine amicably with the very man he has marked for death. By working out some of the ironies, we may understand the function of these two asides. Shakespeare pairs Trebonius with Brutus in order to demonstrate how "All the conspirators save only" Brutus "Did that they did in envy of great Caesar" (5.5.69–70).

The asides tend to draw the audience into the play, as embattled characters solicit approval and support. To whom else but the audience is Cordelia appealing in her first aside in *King Lear:* "What shall Cordelia speak? Love, and be silent" (1.1.61)? Her question and answer exist outside the rhetorical love-match that her pampered and cosseted old father is now conducting. Cordelia's confidential first words in the play are totally unexpected. They emphasize for us the fulsomeness of Goneril's answer to Lear's contest question: "Which of you shall we say doth love us most?" (50). Cordelia's second speech is also spoken aside, just after her sister Regan's empty hyperboles:

> Then poor Cordelia!
> And yet not so; since I am sure my love's
> More ponderous than my tongue.

$$(1.1.75–77)$$

"Ponderous" means weighty and substantial, and it immediately indicates a tragic conflict between love in the heart and love on the tongue. Cordelia's asides are a justification for her kind of love. Without them, her first bits of dialogue—"Nothing, my lord" (86), "Nothing" (88)—would be as incomprehensible to the audience as they are to Lear. Cordelia needs the asides as a way of commenting on the action without engaging in dialogue. Admittedly, they are abrupt and unmotivated, yet the convention allows the dramatist to work boldly and intensely and to spare us a good deal of expository effort.

The asides in *Hamlet* are so abrupt that they are one of the most disturbing features of the play. Suddenly, without any warning, we discover that Claudius is a villain with a conscience. In Ophelia's decoy scene with Hamlet, Polonius speaks a moral platitude that triggers the King's remorseful admission of guilt:

> *Polonius.* We are oft to blame in this:
> 'Tis too much prov'd, that with devo-
> tion's visage
> And pious action we do sugar o'er
> The devil himself.
> *King.* [*Aside*] O, 'tis too true!
> How smart a lash that speech doth give
> my conscience!
> The harlot's cheek, beautied with
> plast'ring art,
> Is not more ugly to the thing that helps
> it
> Than is my deed to my most painted
> word.
> O heavy burden!

$$(3.1.46–54)$$

We are not supposed to ask why this confessional aside occurs at this point in the action and how it is related to the character of Claudius. We don't expect the King to speak this way, but it is useful, structurally, to have his own testimony about his guilt before Hamlet puts on *The Murder of Gonzago*. The aside offers a convenient opportunity for the villain to confirm our suspicions and to demonstrate that he has a conscience.

Asides are not usually independent speeches in Shakespeare, but rather pithy, ironic comments, and in their simplest form they undercut pretensions or actual falsehoods. Every claim in the first speech of Jack Cade, the leader of the rebellious rabble in *Henry VI, Part II*, is repudiated by the asides of his companions, Dick the Butcher and Smith the Weaver:

> *Cade.* My father was a Mortimer—
> *Dick.* [*Aside*] He was an honest man and a
>   good bricklayer.
> *Cade.* My mother a Plantagenet—
> *Dick.* [*Aside*] I knew her well; she was a
>   midwife.
> *Cade.* My wife descended of the Lacies—
> *Dick.* [*Aside*] She was, indeed, a pedlar's
>   daughter, and sold many laces.
> *Smith.* [*Aside*] But now of late, not able to
>   travel with her furr'd pack, she washes
>   bucks here at home.
>
> (4.2.37–46)

We know that Cade has been trained in his part by the Duke of York, so that we are naturally sympathetic to the deflationary asides. There is, of course, something absurd in the bounce of this dialogue, where the statements are exactly balanced against the replies. This is in the style of Shakespeare's earliest comedies, in which the professional clowns regard all other characters as straight men and insist on their prerogative always to have the last word.

The Poetry of the Theater: Genre, Language, and Imagery

The idea of genre has practical implications, because the audience anticipates a play that will be true to its literary type.

❲ In *Hamlet,* Polonius announces the players who offer their services to the court of Elsinore as if he were their publicity agent: "The best actors in the world, either for tragedy, comedy, history, pastoral, pastoral-comical, historical-pastoral, tragical-historical, tragical-comical-historical-pastoral, scene individable, or poem unlimited" (2.2.392–95). Polonius's categories may be the pedantic meanderings of a would-be critic, yet Shakespeare seems to be amusing himself by cataloguing all the possible Renaissance genres, including some impossibly mixed forms. Comedies, histories, and tragedies are in fact the three divisions into which Shakespeare's collected works are arranged in the First Folio of 1623. Each genre or literary kind has its own separate tradition, so that any particular play may be understood in relation to other plays of a similar type and to possibilities within the genre itself.

We can, for example, study Shakespeare's career as a writer of comedies and look for a pattern of development from the early farces to the middle "problem" plays, and from there to the late romances. We can also compare the range of Shakespearean comedy with that of other Elizabethan dramatists such as Jonson, Dekker, and Heywood.

They were scoring notable successes in the realistic, middle-class comedy of London life, a form in which Shakespeare's only near-experiment is *The Merry Wives of Windsor*, set in Windsor. If we wanted to divide Shakespeare's thirty-eight plays generically, in the manner of Polonius, he emerges strongly as a comic writer, with almost twice as many comedies as either tragedies or histories. But this enumeration is misleading, since Shakespeare likes to work in mixed forms. If the histories and the tragedies contain a great deal of comic material, it is equally true that the comedies and the histories have scenes and characters with tragic overtones.

Genre, then, represents a range of possibilities, within which Shakespeare develops his own idiosyncratic interests. We can imagine his comedies, for example, as a spectrum. At one end is the formal purity of farce, where characterization doesn't matter and plot is all-important. At the other are the "problem" comedies, where Shakespeare's satirical energy and appetite for moral abstractions make them seem close to tragedy in spirit. Between these extremes, Shakespearean comedy celebrates the power of love and beauty, in which all difficulties are dissolved in the feasting, dancing, revelry, marriage, and promise of offspring that bring the plays to a close. Toward the end of his career, Shakespeare's romances show a self-conscious dedication to wonder, admiration, and pastoralism, with their accompanying emphasis on artifice, theatricality, and spectacle. Shakespeare's comedies are marked by an extraordinary verbal exuberance, in which wordplay is a proof of the life force, and the clowns seem to control the action by their wit.

In tragedy, the gamut runs from the cruelty and horrors shown on stage to a sense of metaphysical terror and moral chaos, in which nature is called upon to express tragic meanings. Shakespearean tragedy depends on the ability to depict a convincing evil, but in the last tragedies, virtue and vice are so paradoxically mingled that they lack the clarity of moral vision usually thought essential to tragic effect. Shakespeare's tragic protagonists are not necessarily reflective persons, but they all suffer from the stiffness of their moral integrity. The successful persons in tragedy are always those who are practical and politic and who know how to negotiate their commitments. To go one step further, the most intelligent persons in tragedy seem to be the villains, whose plots conspicuously imitate the playwright's own creativity.

One of the most popular kinds of Elizabethan tragedy was the revenge play, and it illustrates the relationship between the traditions of a genre (or subgenre) and the ways in which a playwright could experiment with established patterns. The audience needed no literary sophistication to know that revenge plays follow a certain course: the hidden crime must be revealed, the revenger must be stirred from his lethargy to act, the guilty must be destroyed with ingenious skill, and the revenger himself must eventually be the victim of his own overreaching plot. Not every revenge play pursues the same formula, but the movement is always from revelation to revenge, a process in which delay is implicit. There is nothing unique about delay in *Hamlet*, although Hamlet may be the most self-conscious revenger in Elizabethan drama. The audience at a revenge play is ready for a certain kind of development. It has a feeling for the genre pattern, just as we have some preliminary insight into westerns, spy thrillers, detective stories, and other popular forms. Our insight comes not so much from real life as from reading and seeing other works of the same type.

The history or chronicle play is the most difficult genre to classify—if it is indeed a separate genre at all. The movement in the histories is from strife and civil discord to resolution of conflict, so that their structure is like that of comedy. But Shakespeare is also interested in working out the tragic qualities inherent in the fall of princes. There is no way to apportion shares of comedy and tragedy to the history plays, and one may seize on the notion of a third genre simply out of frustration.

Since the history plays are based on the actual events of the English past, as Shakespeare found them recorded in Holinshed's *Chronicles* and other sources, there is a certain historical sequence that the playwright must follow. The career of Henry V, for example, especially his famous victories in France, was so well known to Elizabethan audiences that no playwright could deviate from its inevitable unfolding. Audiences would not cavil with changes in chronology, minor characters, and general emphasis, nor would they object to anachronistic flourishes, such as King John's defiance of the Pope (in *King John*), or the hatred of England's traditional enemies, especially France and Spain. But what had to remain intact was the chronicle of great princes, heroic battles, and momentous events of state. There is often some intractable material in Shakespeare's history plays that might have disappeared if these plays were conceived as fictions. The beginning of *Henry V* has an extraordinarily prolix explanation of why the Law Salique does not bar Henry from his claim to France. It is not until the very end of Act I, when Henry hurls defiance at the French ambassadors, that *Henry V* begins to come alive, which is surprising in a play that is otherwise so animated, so hearty, and so uncomplicated.

Of the ten histories, all except *King John* and *Henry VIII* fall into sequences usually called the Minor and the Major Tetralogies. The Minor Tetralogy includes the three parts of *Henry VI* and *Richard III*. The Major Tetralogy begins with *Richard II*, continues with the two parts of *Henry IV*, and concludes with *Henry V*. Although each of the eight plays is a separate entity not dependent on any other to complete its meaning, the tetralogies do seem to be the product of a conscious intention. There are, for example, many anticipations of later plays in earlier ones, and there is a striking continuity and consistency of characters within each tetralogy. Richard, Duke of Gloucester, is developed with a view to his later importance as Richard III, and we begin to hear of Prince Hal, who is to become Henry V, as early as *Richard II*. Lesser characters such as Hastings and Northumberland are also interwoven into the whole of their respective sequences. Recollections of previous events have a similar cumulative function. Margaret, the Queen of Henry VI, keeps reappearing as a kind of Nemesis in the Minor Tetralogy to remind us of all the gruesome murders, and in the Major Tetralogy we are never allowed to forget the killing of Richard II by which Henry IV establishes his reign. His son, Henry V, must atone for his father's guilty conscience.

Structurally, it is notable that the first three plays of each tetralogy have weak and inconclusive endings, while the last play in each sequence (*Richard III* and *Henry* V) serves as a climax in which the dramatic issues of the earlier plays are resolved. In *Richard III*, the defeat of Richard brings Henry Tudor, Earl of Richmond, to the throne as Henry VII, and he unifies the houses of York and Lancaster by marriage. The play ends with a vision of the peace and prosperity that the Tudors will bring to England. In *Henry* V, the victory in France seems to remove the stain of Henry IV's ascent to the throne through "by-paths and indirect crook'd ways" (2 *Henry IV* 4.5. 185). By subduing the rebels at home, Henry V asserts his own strong, *de facto* claim to be king, and his reign is a brilliant moment for England.

Although Shakepeare's comedies, tragedies, and histories are not exclusive, self-contained categories, genre is still a significant concept, because it establishes patterns of movement and expectation. In tragicomedy, for example, the events of the plot may be tragic, but the movement of the action is always comic. There is an unmistakably comic or tragic tone that we should be able to distinguish from the beginning of a play. In the histories, the objective, panoramic presentation is perhaps something distinctly different from either comedy or tragedy. The most persuasive argument for genre is to look at it from the dramatist's point of view. Shakespeare wrote such a wide variety of plays not just to satisfy the current fashion (although that motive undoubtedly had force), but also to develop creative opportunities. It seems to me that he was keenly aware of what *kind* of play he was writing, and he relished the ability to do something different within the range of existing types.

*Shakespeare wrote his plays
to be heard rather than
read. His language has the
freedom, irregularity, and
self-indulgence
of spoken English.*

❨ In the Renaissance struggle between the spoken and the written language for preeminence in literature, printing tended to tip the balance toward written forms. By standardizing the wide variety of possible usages, printing acted as a conservative force to slow down the quick pace of linguistic change. By its very existence, it tended to demonstrate and to promote the rules of correctness derived from Latin.

In Shakespeare's lifetime, purists and libertarians were hotly debating the status of the English language, especially its relation to Latin. Some pedants complained about double negatives, double superlatives, inconsistent tenses, and lack of agreement between subject and verb, but grammar, punctuation, spelling, and diction had not yet hardened into a system of prescriptive rules. "This was the most unkindest cut of all" (*Julius Caesar* 3.2.183), says Antony, showing where Brutus stabbed Caesar. It was not only the "unkindest cut," as any of us might presume to say, but "the *most* unkindest cut"—the extra superlative offers a degree of emphasis that has been lost in modern English. Shakespeare and his contemporaries could still think of English as a fluid, changing, developing language that had not yet been fixed. Writers felt free to make up words from Latin roots and to introduce slangy, jargon expressions from daily life.

In the drama, admittedly, the restrictions of decorum apply, and characters from a higher social station use a more formal diction, often heightened by blank verse, whereas clowns and servants are supposed to express themselves in a pungent colloquial, usually in prose. But these distinctions represent general tendencies, and the

social classes in plays cross freely into each other's domains
of usage.

Shakespeare's villains are often his most vivid stylists,
because their villainy allows them to speak their minds
freely and without any intervening formalities. While
Iago, for example, is gulling Roderigo, he scoffs at him
with superb disdain: "I have rubb'd this young quat almost to the sense,/ And he grows angry" (*Othello* 5.1.11–
12). "Quat" is a pimple, a word never used again by Shakespeare and rare in Elizabethan literature. The contemptu-
ous scorn expressed by "quat" is onomatopoetic, and its
emotional tone is plainly evident from its sound. In this
same speech Iago mentions the jewels he has "bobb'd"
(16) from Roderigo as gifts to Desdemona. "Bobb'd"
means stolen and, like "quat," it is a slangy, monosyllabic
word that develops Iago's menace as a villain of daily life.

When one looks at a printed page, the neat arrange-
ment of the words belies their spoken vitality. In speech,
there is a good deal of slurring, and effects of emphasis,
intonation, voice timbre, coloring, and other musical
qualities are totally absent from the regularized, machine-
produced notation of type. Shakespeare's self-indulgent
delight in language for its own sake is a quality almost
lost in modern English style. We have been taught to
write tersely, succinctly, and perspicuously, and to avoid
all traces of artful self-consciousness and self-dramatiza-
tion. But Shakespeare uses language very ostentatiously to
prove the omnipotence of wit. Comic exuberance is
usually expressed by verbal exuberance, and his great
comic figures are primarily great talkers, even great mono-
logists, whom no one can silence, embarrass, put down,
or have the last word with.

Love's Labour's Lost, an early courtly comedy in the
manner of John Lyly, offers the best examples of this sort
of extravagance. Shakespeare presents three pedants in
affectionate, satirical detail, all of whom display some
special, idiosyncratic madness in the use of language.
There are the fantastical, affected Spaniard, Don Armado;
the schoolmaster Holofernes; and his admiring friend, Sir

Nathaniel the curate. As Moth, the witty page says of them: "They have been at a great feast of languages and stol'n the scraps" (5.1.33–34), and Costard the clown answers with becoming polysyllabeity: "I marvel thy master hath not eaten thee for a word, for thou are not so long by the head as honorificabilitudinitatibus" (36–38). This is probably an ironic allusion to the boy Moth's tiny stature.

For these pedants, refined diction is itself the object of their discourse, without any base ulterior motive of communication. In his effort to scale the heights of polite circumlocution, Don Armado finds it almost impossible to convey mere facts: "Sir, it is the King's most sweet pleasure and affection to congratulate the Princess at her pavilion, in the posteriors of this day; which the rude multitude call the afternoon" (74–77). To which Holofernes replies with the admiration of one professional for another: "The posterior of the day, most generous sir, is liable, congruent, and measurable, for the afternoon. The word is well cull'd, chose, sweet, and apt, I do assure you, sir, I do assure" (78–81). But of course the rude multitude would interpret "posteriors" in a sense different from that of Don Armado and Holofernes.

The character of Pistol, the swaggering companion of Falstaff in *Henry IV, Part II*, is almost entirely conceived as a vehicle for verbal display. Without his parodies of the heroic high style, Pistol ceases to exist, and his name, as Falstaff is constantly reminding him, makes a familiar pun on "pizzle" (the penis of an animal, especially a bull). In the scene at the Boar's Head Tavern in Eastcheap, when Falstaff is making himself comfortable with Doll Tearsheet and Mistress Quickly—names that also suggest obscene puns—Falstaff is anxious to be rid of the intrusive Pistol: "No more, Pistol; I would not have you go off here. Discharge yourself of our company, Pistol" (2.4.127–29). And Falstaff refers to the aging Mistress Quickly as "pistol-proof" (110).

As a dramatic speaker, Pistol confines himself to the words of others, especially the "high astounding terms" he has heard at the playhouse. In the lines that follow, he

is not only parodying the grandiloquent vaunting of Mar-
lowe's Tamburlaine of a decade earlier, but also the rant-
ing tyrant's style of plays of the mid-sixteenth century
such as Thomas Preston's *Cambises: A Lamentable Tragedy Mixed Full of Pleasant Mirth*. Pistol waxes wroth in
what Falstaff calls "King Cambyses' vein" (1 *Henry IV*
2.4.376):

> Shall packhorses,
> And hollow pamper'd jades of Asia,
> Which cannot go but thirty mile a day,
> Compare with Caesars, and with Cannibals,
> And Troiant Greeks? Nay, rather damn
> them with
> King Cerberus; and let the welkin roar.
> (2 *Henry IV* 2.4.154–59)

Although his "Cannibals" is a happy blunder for "Hanni-
bals," Pistol is clearly a name-dropper, and he intends to
strike terror into his hearers when he refers to his sword
with a literary flourish: "Have we not Hiren here?" (165).
No one on stage seems much perturbed by the threatening
presence of Hiren, or Irene, which Pistol probably pro-
nounced Cockney-style as "iron."

The relatively minor role of Pistol makes us aware of
the enormous resources of wordplay in Shakespeare. It
is not just the idle curiosity of scholars that has discovered
in the text double, triple, and quadruple meanings, many
of which are likely to be of impertinent connotation. The
puns are often more apparent to the ear than to the eye,
as in Hamlet's lewd taunt to Ophelia in the play scene:
"Do you think I meant *country* matters?" (3.2.112). One
of Hamlet's primary roles is as a punster. His first utter-
ances in the play are a string of satirical, bitter puns:
Claudius is "less than kind"(= both "gentle" and "natural"); Hamlet is "too much in the sun" (= "son");
death in Gertrude's description is "common" (= "ordinary" but also "vulgar"); and Hamlet declares that he
knows not "seems," which is not only seeming, but also
the seamy side of the garment, and the same hog's fat
(or "seam") that makes the "rank sweat of an enseamed

bed" (3.4.92). As Polonius says of him, nursing wounds of Hamlet's making: "How pregnant sometimes his replies are" (2.2.208). These examples should suggest that word-play is not restricted to Shakespeare's comedies. It is also an essential feature of his tragic art, which relies on grotesque contrasts between jest and earnest, as shown by the gravediggers in *Hamlet* and the Fool in *King Lear*. Wordplay calls attention to the complexity of language in the tragedies, where the words seem to have an unpredictable life of their own.

Perhaps it would be more just to say that the omnipresence of wordplay in Shakespeare offers a way of breaking down artificial distinctions between comedy and tragedy. In *Antony and Cleopatra,* for example, Cleopatra's sophisticated *double-entendres* illuminate her tragic role. Her scene with the eunuch Mardian early in the play establishes Cleopatra's trenchant wit as well as the atmosphere of boredom from which it develops. Cleopatra gives all of Mardian's words a devastating sexual twist. "What's your Highness' pleasure?" (1.5.8), says he in a neutral formula of service, to which Cleopatra replies with cutting scorn: "Not now to hear thee sing; I take no pleasure/ In aught an eunuch has" (9–10). And Mardian, picking up Cleopatra's cue, interprets her "Indeed?" as a sexual pun: "Not in deed, madam; for I can do nothing/ But what indeed is honest to be done" (15–16). The upshot of this mood comes in Cleopatra's vision of the absent Antony on horseback: "O happy horse, to bear the weight of Antony!" (21). Cleopatra has the same furious jealousy of that horse as she does of Fulvia, Antony's Roman wife in this part of the play.

Language is treacherous in Shakespeare, and once we become aware of wordplay, it is difficult to read almost any passage without being conscious of multiple meanings. There is probably more bawdy in Shakespeare than even the industrious Eric Partridge could find in his book, *Shakespeare's Bawdy.* If *Romeo and Juliet* celebrates the beauty and grace of young love, it is also, in its language, Shakespeare's dirtiest play. The grossness of the Nurse is essential for understanding the luminous innocence of Juliet, and Mercutio's witty pornography sets off the intensity of Romeo's commitment. In the heroic, epic world of *Henry V*, we are convinced that Katherine, his French bride-to-be, is not just a puppet of dynastic ambitions, but a charming, passionate girl eager for marriage. Her language lesson in English (3.4) is spiced with bawdy touches. When she asks innocently: "Comment appelez-vous le pied et la robe?" (45–46)—"What's the English for foot and dress?," her instructress replies: "Le foot, madame; et le count" (46). "Foot" in the French pronunciation (= *foutre*) is a gross obscenity, and "count," a Gallic attempt at "gown," is a dirty word in French (= *con*) or English. Katherine amusingly protests against the omnipresence of four-letter words in English; it is apparently not a language that modest maidens can use in public.

A language lesson is the basis for what is perhaps the bawdiest dialogue in all of Shakespeare: the instruction in Latin that Sir Hugh Evans, the Welsh schoolmaster, gives to young William Page in *The Merry Wives of Windsor*, with the learned commentary of Mistress Quickly, quondam proprietress of the Boar's Head Tavern in Eastcheap and now the honorable wife of Signor Pistol. With his inimitable Welsh accent, Evans demands to know the "focative case" (4.1.46) of the definite article— a trap question, since "focative is caret" or lacking, but one which rouses Mistress Quickly's enthusiasm: "And that's a good root" (49). In the discussion of the genitive case, she can no longer restrain her indignation that it should be "horum, harum, horum"; "Vengeance of Jenny's case; fie on her! Never name her, child, if she be a whore" (56–57). One needs to know that "case" was a canting word for what Havelock Ellis used to call the "pudendum," but the whore's name Jenny can only be derived from "genitive" by appealing to the oral tradition. Mistress Quickly puts herself in the venerable company of those who satirize pedantry, and she sharpens our awareness of ambiguities in the basic curriculum.

*An author's imagery reveals
his symbolic preoccupations
and expresses an imagin-
ative coherence
in the world of the play.*

❴ Shakespeare's imagery has aroused interest in recent years, because the image patterns seem to delineate a subterranean play different from the public document. The imagery, especially in the tragedies, indicates what is going on beneath the surface of plot and character. In its widest meaning, imagery is the equivalent of the art historian's iconography and includes all the means of symbolization in any work. Images may be found not just in figures of speech, but also in references to a certain subject matter, no matter how unimportant their immediate context. In studying plays, we must also consider the nonverbal imagery of costumes, properties, and sound effects that is directly presented in the dramatic action. We need to assume that the effect of imagery is cumulative. We may not be aware that an image is important until it begins to impress itself on us by repetition. Once a pattern is felt to exist, all the examples interrelate with each other. This may be difficult to see in a play, because, unlike a printed book, it progresses temporally outside of our control—we cannot stop or slow down the play for the sake of the image patterns. Yet even in a performance, the images are seeded in the mind and work their effects with a gradual but sure emphasis.

Certain images are repeated so often in Shakespeare that they function as a special symbolic language. The imagery of disease, for example, is negative because it is connected with ugliness, disorder, discord, and evil. In the history plays, the whole body of England may be distempered, a radical condition that can only be cured by war. If the nation is diseased, then all of nature responds sympathetically. Analogies may be drawn between the body of an individual (usually the king), the body politic, and the world's body, and our responses are conditioned by our readiness for these symbolic correspondences. In *King John*, for example, the raging death of the King by poison is taken to be a judgment on his political as well as his personal life:

> Within me is a hell; and there the poison
> Is as a fiend confin'd to tyrannize
> On unreprievable condemned blood.
>   (5.7.46–48)

We have much the same feeling about the death of King Henry IV, who, in his illness, thinks of those "by-paths and indirect crook'd ways" by which he gained the crown (*2 Henry IV* 4.5.185). And the "crafty-sick" Northumberland represents the actual sickness of the conspiracy, both in itself and in its relation to the health of England.

The disease imagery in the tragedies follows the pattern of the history plays. Macbeth, for example, immediately analogizes the sickness of his Queen:

> If thou couldst, doctor, cast
> The water of my land, find her disease,
> And purge it to a sound and pristine health,
> I would applaud thee to the very echo,
> That should applaud again . . . .
> What rhubarb, senna, or what purgative
>   drug,
> Would scour these English hence?
>   (5.3.50–56)

By its traditional application, the imagery of disease has a moral function.

Animal imagery has the same negative reference as that of disease. The basic notion is that man, endowed with the godlike faculty of reason, should be superior to animals, who are governed by instinctive drives and appetites. There are noble animals in Shakespeare (the lion and the eagle) and gentle ones (the lamb and the dove), but animals are generally associated with grossness, aggression, and ravening prey.

Of all Shakespeare's characters, Richard III is defined most consistently in animal terms. His own mother reproaches herself for giving birth to such a venomous creature:

> O my accursed womb, the bed of death!
> A cockatrice hast thou hatch'd to the world,
> Whose unavoided eye is murderous.
>
> (4.1.54–56)

A cockatrice is a basilisk, a fabled serpent with a killing look. The grieving Queen Margaret expresses the same idea in a dog image:

> From forth the kennel of thy womb hath crept
> A hell-hound that doth hunt us all to death.
> That dog, that had his teeth before his eyes
> To worry lambs and lap their gentle blood . . . .
>
> (4.4.47–50)

Richard is also called a "poisonous bunch-back'd toad" (1.3.246), a "bottled spider" (1.3.242), an "elvish-mark'd, abortive, rooting hog" (1.3.228), a "wretched, bloody, and usurping boar" (5.2.7), a hedgehog, a tiger, and a wolf. The repulsiveness of the animal imagery is strengthened by Richard's appearance; his physical deformity expresses his bestial nature.

The imagery of food and eating calls attention to man's appetites, one of his strongest links with the animals. Often the food images are also animal images, as in the closet scene of *Hamlet*, where the Prince shows his mother the portraits of his father and his uncle and asks incredulously: "Could you on this fair mountain leave to feed,/ And batten on this moor?" (3.4.66–67). There is a pun on "moor" as a swampland and as an ugly, dark-skinned person, and "batten" is a specific word for animal feeding. This appetitive imagery is used most often for sensuality. Cleopatra may be a "dish for the gods" (5.2.273), but in a different mood Antony describes her in images of disgusting bits of food:

> I found you as a morsel cold upon
> Dead Caesar's trencher. Nay, you were a fragment

Of Cneius Pompey's, besides what hotter
  hours,
Unregist'red in vulgar fame, you have
Luxuriously pick'd out . . . .

(3.13.116–20)

This kind of imagery enters most powerfully into the world of *Troilus and Cressida*, where it works together with the references to disease and animals. At the beginning of the play, Pandarus represents the pursuit of Cressida in the *double-entendres* of food preparation:

> *Pandarus*. He that will have a cake out of
>   the wheat must needs tarry the
>   grinding.
> *Troilus*. Have I not tarried?
> *Pandarus*. Ay, the grinding; but you must
>   tarry the bolting.
> *Troilus*. Have I not tarried?
> *Pandarus*. Ay, the bolting; but you must
>   tarry the leavening.
> *Troilus*. Still have I tarried.
> *Pandarus*. Ay, to the leavening; but here's yet
>   in the word 'hereafter' the kneading,
>   the making of the cake, the heating of
>   the oven, and the baking; nay, you
>   must stay the cooling too, or you may
>   chance to burn your lips.

(1.1.15–26)

This is one of the most openly leering passages in Shakespeare, and Pandarus delights in his witty figure. It is appropriate, therefore, that Troilus's disillusion should also be expressed in the imagery of food:

> The bonds of heaven are slipp'd, dissolv'd,
>   and loos'd;
> And with another knot, five-finger-tied,
> The fractions of her faith, orts of her love,
> The fragments, scraps, the bits, and greasy
>   relics
> Of her o'er-eaten faith, are bound to
>   Diomed.

(5.2.154–58)

As in Antony's representation of Cleopatra, the images are drawn from the leftovers after a meal, which are fed to dogs or thrown away as garbage.

Disease, animals, and food all offer normative imageries, with fixed moral values that can be evoked almost without any conscious thought by the audience. Similarly, the imagery of light and darkness draws an immediate response, and it can be used to mark stages in the dramatic structure. In its simplest form, night represents the tragic fall and death. There is a very explicit example in Titinius's comments on the dead Cassius:

> O setting sun,
> As in thy red rays thou dost sink to night,
> So in his red blood Cassius' day is set!
> The sun of Rome is set. Our day is gone . . . .
> (*Julius Caesar* 5.3.60–63)

The matching of the parts of the image suggests an exact equivalence in Titinius's mind, as if the language were not figurative at all.

In *Romeo and Juliet*, Juliet's attraction is expressed by the imagery of light. She is a "bright angel" (2.2.26), "she doth teach the torches to burn bright" (1.5.42), and Romeo compares the stars invidiously with her resplendence:

> The brightness of her cheek would shame
>   those stars,
> As daylight doth a lamp; her eyes in heaven
> Would through the airy region stream so
>   bright
> That birds would sing, and think it were not
>   night.
>
> (2.2.19–22)

These are the amorous conceits of the Elizabethan sonneteers, yet Shakespeare manages to endow them with youthful freshness and intensity. Perhaps this imagery is so effective just because it is so familiar; no intellectual effort is required to interpret Romeo's exuberant declarations. To complete the symbolic contrast, the last scene of the play is staged in the torchlight of Juliet's tomb, "this palace of dim night" (5.3.107). The movement from light to dark in *Romeo and Juliet* is a paradigm of tragedy, in which "quick bright things come to confusion" (*A Midsummer Night's Dream* 1.1.149).

The imagery of vertical dimension provides an even simpler structural pattern than light and darkness. In *Richard II*, Richard's fall is set against Bolingbroke's rise, as if they were in inverse relation to each other. When he is deposed, Richard forces his antagonist to hold one side of the crown while he holds the other, so that they may act out a tableau for the King's conceit:

> Now is this golden crown like a deep well
> That owes two buckets, filling one another;
> The emptier ever dancing in the air,
> The other down, unseen, and full of water.
> That bucket down and full of tears am I,
> Drinking my griefs, whilst you mount up on
>   high.
>
> (4.1.184–89)

Richard works out all the parts of the analogy, which makes his figure completely pictorial.

In answer to Northumberland's request for him to come down to the base court, Richard expatiates on the image of vertical dimension:

> Down, down I come, like glist'ring
>   Phaethon,
> Wanting the manage of unruly jades.
> In the base court? Base court, where kings
>   grow base,
> To come at traitors' calls, and do them
>   grace.
> In the base court? Come down? Down,
>   court! down, king!
> For night-owls shriek where mounting larks
>   should sing.
>
> (3.3.178–83)

The imagery also indicates Richard's descent from the upper stage. Again, when Bolingbroke kneels to him, Richard sees in this action a false relationship:

> Up, cousin, up; your heart is up, I know,
> [*Touching his own head*] Thus high at least,
> although your knee be low.
>
> (3.3.194–95)

The demonstrative imagery emphasizes points that are also being made by gesture.

Imagery plays a decisive role in indicating tone, mood, or atmosphere. As readers of Shakespeare, we need to know not only what the words mean, but also how we should interpret them. Speakers of the most fastidious morality may be harsh and manipulative in their tone, and the villains in Shakespeare are usually most concerned with maintaining public appearances. The imagery imparts a distinctive coloring to the tone, so that we will not take characters at their own face value, or be misled by the literal meaning of their words.

The presented poetry of a play is essentially different from lyric poetry on the printed page.

❲ If Shakespeare had written no plays at all, his lyric poetry would still be a remarkable achievement. *Venus and Adonis* is much admired for its witty, amorous style in the tradition of Ovid, and Shakespeare's sonnets are notable for their combination of passionate eloquence and epigrammatic precision. There is also the brief threnody of "The Phoenix and the Turtle," celebrating the power of love in an elusive symbolism. The moralism of the long narrative poem, *The Rape of Lucrece*, is less admired by modern readers, but it does contain some splendid stanzas on the Trojan War (lines 1366ff.). Shakespeare's nondramatic writings have thematic links with his plays, and in *Venus and Adonis* there is a strong feeling that the scenes and the characters are dramatically conceived. Yet *Venus and Adonis* as a lyric poem is essentially different from anything in the plays, and it is worth insisting on this difference in order to understand Shakespeare's dramatic poetry.

As an experiment, we may try setting a passage from *Venus and Adonis* side by side with a passage from *Romeo and Juliet,* both of which use the conventions of love in a fairly artificial way. The love plea of Venus early in the poem is not unlike Romeo's first wooing of Juliet, although Romeo as a character is closer to Adonis than to the mature, sophisticated, and even lubricious Venus. In a formal and highly rhetorical argument, Venus tries to entrap Adonis into amorous sport:

> 'Touch but my lips with those fair lips of
> thine;
> Though mine be not so fair, yet are they
> red—
> The kiss shall be thine own as well as mine.
> What seest thou in the ground? Hold up
> thy head;
> Look in mine eyeballs; there thy beauty
> lies.
> Then why not lips on lips, since eyes in
> eyes?
>
> 'Art thou asham'd to kiss? Then wink again,
> And I will wink; so shall the day seem
> night.
> Love keeps his revels where there are but
> twain;
> Be bold to play; our sport is not in sight.
> These blue-vein'd violets whereon we lean
> Never can blab, nor know not what we
> mean.'
>
> (115–26)

In both poem and play, witty artifice expresses erotic purpose, and plain-speaking sincerity would only be a sign of dullness. Like Venus, Romeo woos "by th' book," which seems to mean that he speaks more from the manuals of love etiquette than from the heart. Juliet of course replies in the appropriate style of enticing modesty. In their first speech together at Capulet's ball, they answer each other in an artful sonnet of four quatrains and a concluding couplet, with another quatrain added at the end:

> *Romeo.* If I profane with my unworthiest
>   hand
>   This holy shrine, the gentle fine is this:
>   My lips, two blushing pilgrims, ready
>   stand
>   To smooth that rough touch with a
>   tender kiss.
> *Juliet.* Good pilgrim, you do wrong your
>   hand too much,
>   Which mannerly devotion shows in
>   this;
>   For saints have hands that pilgrims'
>   hands do touch,
>   And palm to palm is holy palmers' kiss.
> *Romeo.* Have not saints lips, and holy
>   palmers too?
> *Juliet.* Ay, pilgrim, lips that they must use
>   in pray'r.
> *Romeo.* O, then, dear saint, let lips do what
>   hands do!
>   They pray; grant thou, lest faith turn
>   to despair.
> *Juliet.* Saints do not move, though grant for
>   prayers' sake.
> *Romeo.* Then move not while my prayer's
>   effect I take.
>   Thus from my lips by thine my sin is
>   purg'd. [*Kissing her.*]
> *Juliet.* Then have my lips the sin that they
>   have took.
> *Romeo.* Sin from my lips? O trespass sweetly
>   urg'd!
>   Give me my sin again. [*Kissing her.*]
> *Juliet.*   You kiss by th' book.
>   (1.5.91–108)

This may seem like lyric poetry on the printed page, yet the sonnet has a dramatic context that is entirely lacking in *Venus and Adonis*. The gestural language in *Romeo and Juliet* is an intrinsic part of the lovers' poetizing.

"This holy shrine" is, of course, Juliet's hand, which is enclasped "palm to palm" in a "holy palmer's kiss"—a verbal and a visual pun—with Romeo's hand. There is another pun on "move," when Romeo wishes Juliet to stay still while he kisses her. We are not allowed to forget that no matter how ardent the lovers are, they are also actors trying to perform the stage business with becoming elegance. In the larger context of the tragedy, Romeo and Juliet never court each other again in this affected style. There is something self-indulgent about the scene at the ball, as if Romeo had not fully recovered from his previous affair with Rosaline. By the time of the "balcony" scene (2.2), everything has changed. This sort of contextual approach is not relevant to *Venus and Adonis*. Even though it narrates a series of events in time, these events are not dramatized. The poem has a much narrower stylistic purpose than *Romeo and Juliet*, and it achieves the sort of unity of mood, tone, and setting that is not possible in a play.

Because the poetic effects Shakespeare aims at in his plays are so different from those of lyric poetry, the great dramatic moments are sometimes difficult to recognize out of context. Lear's "Pray you undo this button" (5.3.309) may in itself seem banal or even bathetic, but in the old king's final speech it has an electrifying effect. He has entered this scene with the dead Cordelia in his arms, and now at the end he cannot understand why, in the nature of things, should "a dog, a horse, a rat have life,/ And thou no breath at all" (306–7). This is the final, inscrutable mystery:

> Thou'lt come no more,
> Never, never, never, never, never.
> Pray you undo this button. Thank you, sir.
> (5.3.307–9)

Lear's part ends with the illusion of Cordelia's breathing, but there are no comforting assurances. As Kent says, "All's cheerless, dark, and deadly" (290). Lear's "Pray you undo this button" suggests a feeling of suffocation, and it seems to echo the earlier "Off, off, you lendings!

Come, unbutton here" (3.4.107–8), by which Lear asserts his kinship with naked, "unaccommodated man" (105).

The greatness of *King Lear* probably depends more directly on these eloquent flashes of dramatic poetry than any other play of Shakespeare. Cordelia's exclamation, "And so I am, I am" (4.7.70), for example, is one of the most moving lines in the play, although it has no intrinsic interest at all out of context. Cordelia has been reunited with her father, whose madness she ministers to by the restoratives of sleep and music. As Lear in "fresh garments" (22) awakes, he thinks himself in hell,

> bound
> Upon a wheel of fire, that mine own tears
> Do scald like molten lead.
>
> (4.7.46–48)

He is dazed in spirit and cannot recognize either his daughter or himself. To Cordelia, this is a bitter disappointment, but she perseveres in her desire to have her father's blessing:

> O, look upon me, sir,
> And hold your hands in benediction o'er me.
> No, sir, you must not kneel.
>
> (4.7.57–59)

Through a series of slow identifications, Lear begins to put the pieces of his life together, and he comes hesitantly and tentatively to a conclusion that he cannot believe possible:

> Do not laugh at me;
> For, as I am a man, I think this lady
> To be my child Cordelia.
>
> (4.7.68–70)

It is at this triumphant recognition that Cordelia says: "And so I am, I am" (70). This is her great moment of assertion, the climax of an overwhelming emotional pressure, and radically different from her first public words in the play: "Nothing, my lord" (1.1.86). Lear and Cordelia will soon be captured by Edmund (5.3), so that the reunion of father and daughter in Act IV, scene vii, is only a momentary illusion of happiness.

Shakespeare sometimes uses the techniques of lyric poetry in his plays to make some special point about a character. Richard II, for example, is developed as a minor poet, which raises the fascinating question of how a first-rate dramatist goes about portraying a second-rate poet. In this play there is a strong emphasis on Richard's fanciful, far-fetched, ingenious comparisons—what Renaissance rhetoricians called "conceits." Richard poetizes in the style of an overly enthusiastic metaphysical poet: he is so preoccupied with his strained analogies and subtle wordplay that his images tend to be unrelated to the point they are expected to illustrate, and the emotional tone is either false or grotesque. At the moment when we expect Richard to be exhorting his troops to do battle against Bolingbroke, the King is spinning out a pretty invocation of the baleful powers of nature. He calls for "spiders" and "heavy-gaited toads" to impede the "usurping steps" (3.2.14,15,17) of his enemy, and once he embarks on the figure, he works out its symbolic details with aesthetic relish. Richard's poetizing is used pejoratively to assure us that he cannot possibly resist Bolingbroke and continue as king. It is only when Richard is deposed that his lyric poetry begins to justify itself as an expression of tragic pathos.

Shakespeare's Characters: Style and Morality

*Shakespeare's heroines may be
simpler and more virtuous
than we have been taught
to believe . . .*

❲ As readers of Shakespeare, we have been trained to
hunt for psychological complexity in his characters, as
if complexity were in itself the highest value both in literature and in life. This pursuit is part of that unfortunate
Victorian legacy of "character analysis," in which the
motives of dramatic persons were rigorously scrutinized by
the criteria of daily life. But characters in a play are imag-
inatively conceived, and Shakespeare's characters exist in
a context of moral conventions which tend to simplify
their psychological motivation. It is sometimes necessary
to assume an absolute degree of good or evil in a Shakespearean character, as in morality plays and folk tales,
and to allow for abrupt shifts in character that violate
logical progression. In order to read Shakespeare in his
own terms, we must be willing to accept dramatic persons
who are frankly rhetorical and discontinuous.

In *Othello*, for example, Desdemona cannot possibly
be a rounded and multidimensional character like a
heroine in a nineteenth-century novel. She is presented
boldly and clearly and without any moral equivocation;
her innocence is not in any way qualified or put into
question during the play. It is crucial for understanding
the tragedy that there be no basis at all for Othello's

75

jealousy. When he enters his wife's bedchamber to strangle her, his first words hypnotically assert his commitment to a cause-and-effect morality:

> It is the cause, it is the cause, my soul—
> Let me not name it to you, you chaste stars—
> It is the cause.
>
> (5.2.1–3)

But there is no "cause," as Othello is soon to discover. Desdemona's adultery is all a cunning illusion by which Iago has ensnared the gullible Moor, and that is the point of Othello's tragedy.

By virtue of dramatic irony, we are able to see beyond Othello's limited perspective, and we are always aware of what Iago is doing. Yet even though we are certain that Iago is a villain, we find ourselves being insidiously persuaded by the invented details of Desdemona's affair with Cassio. Against our better judgment, we share Othello's tragic credulity, by which we show our natural preference for complex explanations of character and motive rather than simple ones. Iago can exist only because the truth has always been so difficult to believe. But the action in *Othello* assumes that Desdemona is completely innocent of Iago's insinuations, just as Hermione in *The Winter's Tale* offers no basis at all for her husband's self-generated jealousy.

Desdemona's scene with Emilia shortly before Desdemona is murdered in her bed is meant to insist once more on her absolute innocence. Iago's wife is a woman of this world: practical, prudent, unheroic, full of common sense and shrewd insight. When Desdemona questions her about the nature of virtue and vice, Emilia answers with honest, workaday wisdom:

> *Desdemona.* Dost thou in conscience think
> —tell me, Emilia—
> That there be women do abuse their
> husbands
> In such gross kind?

Emilia. There be some such, no question.
Desdemona. Wouldst thou do such a deed
    for all the world?
Emilia. Why, would not you?
Desdemona. No, by this heavenly light!
Emilia. Nor I neither by this heavenly light;
    I might do't as well i' th' dark.

(4.3.59–65)

Emilia is in an entirely different world of discourse from Desdemona, and she can only interpret her questions with amused detachment. Desdemona seems to understand nothing of what Emilia is saying; she asks her again, with incredulity: "Wouldst thou do such a deed for all the world?" (66). Emilia says yes in as gentle a way as she knows: "The world's a huge thing./ It is a great price for a small vice" (67–68). The "price-vice" jingle suggests a certain triviality in what Emilia is saying, but Desdemona refuses to believe her: "Good troth, I think thou wouldst not" (69), and later she affirms: "I do not think there is any such woman" (81). Desdemona is incapable of acknowledging the existence of evil, and it is her unsophisticated purity that makes her so vulnerable to Othello's attack. If she will not be persuaded by Emilia's affable demonstration that adultery exists, how can she possibly understand Iago's calumny? In some sense, then, both Desdemona and Othello are innocents who suffer because they cannot comprehend the evil that surrounds them.

Hamlet's "fair Ophelia" has generated even more idle gossip than Desdemona. There is nothing in the play to support the notions that she has been having an affair with Claudius, or that she has been gotten with child by Hamlet, gone mad for grief, and committed suicide to avoid the shame. These malicious explanations are designed to make Ophelia into a more complex character than she is in the play. Her simplicity baffles us. Unless we believe Ophelia completely innocent, her mad scene has no dramatic purpose. Her distracted bawdiness there is the direct antitype of her constrained virginity earlier,

and her snatches of mad songs express the wish-fulfill-
ment of comedy:

> Then up he rose, and donn'd his clothes,
>   And dupp'd [= opened] the chamber-door;
> Let in the maid, that out a maid
>   Never departed more.
>
> (4.5.50–53)

It is also remarkable how deliberately Ophelia is detached
from her father's plots, even those in which she participates. When the decoy scene with Hamlet is concluded,
she is brushed aside as the merest factotum by Polonius:

> How now, Ophelia!
> You need not tell us what Lord Hamlet said;
> We heard it all.
>
> (3.1.178–80)

Shakespeare seems determined to protect Ophelia from
any taint of corruption.

. . . and his villains often express pure, unmotivated evil.

❡ The malevolence of Shakespeare's villains is difficult to
account for either by their past history or by their present
grievances. Shakespeare wants to avoid giving them a
believable background that would justify or explain their
evil. The villains are generally not motivated at all—at
least not by detective-story standards—but are presented
to us already securely entrenched in their moral condition.
Their evil is a positive and active force, and its unques-
tioned energy makes the villains seem diabolic. We need
to accept them as they appear without probing the origins
of their conduct. This requires forbearance from the
audience, whose love of scandalous explanation is deliberately frustrated.

What are we to make of the reasons Iago offers for his
savage revenge on Othello? Is he acting from thwarted
ambition, because Cassio has the promotion Iago thinks

he himself deserves? Or are the reasons more subtle and more personal? As Iago tells us,

> I hate the Moor;
> And it is thought abroad that 'twixt my
>   sheets
> 'Has done my office. I know not if't be true;
> Yet I, for mere suspicion in that kind,
> Will do as if for surety.
>
> (1.3.380–84)

There is a cynical coldness in "I know not if't be true," and Iago never troubles himself to find out. Personal honor means nothing to him, since in his view all women are whores and all human activity is base, coarse, gross, and disgusting. What is important is that Iago hates the Moor. That is enough, and reasons are alleged merely to satisfy public opinion.

In a much-quoted phrase, Coleridge spoke of this aspect of Iago's morality as the "motive-hunting of motiveless malignity." In other words, there are no motives and there is no cause that can account for Iago's evil. Othello never understands this, because even at the very end of the play he still wants to learn from that "demi-devil" "Why he hath thus ensnar'd my soul and body" (5.2.305). But Iago refuses any final comforts for Othello's tragic rationalism: "Demand me nothing. What you know, you know./ From this time forth I never will speak word" (306–7). Ultimately, there can be no answer to Othello's question. We have only a hint of explanation when Iago justifies the murder of Cassio: "He hath a daily beauty in his life/ That makes me ugly" (5.1.19–20). This judgment has the true satanic ring. Like Lucifer, Iago is irresistibly attracted to the beauty from which he has been excluded for all eternity, and this sense of damnation makes his revenge so monomaniacal.

Iago is Shakespeare's most brilliant villain, who dominates his play in a way no other villain can (except perhaps Macbeth, a villain-hero). He forces us to consider one of the most difficult paradoxes of tragedy: Why is the villain usually so much more intelligent, insightful, sensitive, and imaginative than his victim? The villain seems to be the surrogate for the diabolic-creative powers of the dramatist. Iago is wonderfully complex in his manipulation of the dramatic action; his plots and Shakespeare's seem to come together, so that one could speak of the stagecraft of villainy and its aesthetics. But in his moral nature Iago is wonderfully simple, if not actually simplified. The presence of both Iago and Desdemona in a single play assumes that good and evil exist as warring postulates. This is the morality play aspect of Shakespearean tragedy.

Similarly, in *King Lear* we are not meant to discuss the characters of Goneril and Regan as if they were actual persons with mixed virtues and vices. They are not mixed characters at all, but archetypes of the evil daughters, just as Cordelia is the loving daughter who cannot flatter her father. This is the folk-tale proposition with which *Lear* begins. If we insist on pursuing psychological meanings in the play, we will soon find ourselves agreeing with Goneril about Lear's "unruly waywardness that infirm and choleric years bring with them" (1.1.297–98). And of Lear's hundred knights, Regan's question does not seem so unreasonable: "What need one?" (2.4.262). It may appear that the daughters mean to teach their old father a useful lesson by shutting him out on the heath on such a wild night; as Regan says to Gloucester with moral unction:

> O sir, to wilful men
> The injuries that they themselves procure
> Must be their schoolmasters. Shut up your
> doors.
>
> (2.4.301–3)

But this perspective is completely false, because Goneril and Regan are made to seem reasonable and domestic in order to mask their natural depravity. The play is not directed to uncovering a bad family situation. Lear's revelations are about the existence of evil in the world, of man's inhumanity to man, and the play is remarkable for dealing so directly with moral issues of the largest magnitude.

Caliban, the earthy monster of *The Tempest*, also represents a natural evil that cannot be altered by the civilizing influences of education. With our optimistic ideas about human nature, we find it difficult to accept what Shakespeare is telling us about Caliban, but as the drunken scenes with Stephano and Trinculo witness, he is a natural slave. Even Prospero, who is constantly tempering magic with instruction, is not able to achieve any results with Caliban:

> A devil, a born devil, on whose nature
> Nurture can never stick; on whom my pains,
> Humanely taken, all, all lost, quite lost;
> And as with age his body uglier grows,
> So his mind cankers.
>
> (4.1.188–92)

"Nurture" is the Renaissance equivalent of "education" —the opposite of "nature"—but Caliban is beyond redemption. Despite all efforts to improve him, he remains an ugly, misshapen monster, the son of a witch, who is merely acting out his devilish nature. Caliban's response to Prospero's kindness is an attempt to rape Miranda, who, despite her gentleness and admiring innocence, reviles him as "Abhorred slave,/ Which any print of goodness wilt not take" (1.2.351–52). She definitely rules Caliban out of her enumeration of human creatures.

In his physical deformity, Caliban has a certain type relation to the villainous Richard III, who is, by his own boastful admission, "Deform'd, unfinish'd, sent before my time/ Into this breathing world scarce half made up" (*Richard III* 1.1.20–21). Their commitment to evil is a moral assumption of the play—almost an instinct. Not only is no explanation offered for the origin of their evil, but it is made to seem a manifestation of physical repulsiveness. Shakespeare draws on the convenient Platonic assumption that form and content are mutually expressive, so that an ugly body is an outward sign of a vicious soul.

Moral conventions in the presentation of character allow Shakespeare to ignore psychological realities.

❲ Shakespeare's characters are not developed novelistically by accumulating details that lead to one irresistible conclusion. Rather, the characters respond to various dramatic contexts, and therefore they may seem discontinuous or even inconsistent in different parts of the play. Because a play proceeds uninterruptedly as a temporal unit, audiences tend to overlook the sort of character disparities that preoccupy readers, and it is possible for Shakespeare to make unexplained jumps in the logical sequence.

There is an excellent example of this technique in *Coriolanus*, a late tragedy whose superb craftsmanship has been neglected by critics. *Coriolanus* deliberately skips over the most significant character point in the entire play: Why does the protagonist choose to betray his native Rome and fight for her deadly enemy, the Volscians? The question is never answered, and Coriolanus himself seems totally unconcerned about his own motives. There is simply a gap in the dramatic action that Shakespeare did not intend to fill. After Coriolanus is exiled through the machinations of the tribunes, he delivers a ringing exit speech in which he banishes his banishers and threatens vaguely: "There is a world elsewhere" (3.3.137). Act IV begins with Coriolanus taking leave of Rome. Although he goes alone, "Like to a lonely dragon, that his fen/ Makes fear'd and talk'd of more than seen" (4.1.30–31), he does not seem to know where his exile will lead him. We don't get any inkling of what is happening until Act IV, scene iii. Here, too, direct explanation is avoided. From the trivial spy talk of Nicanor and Adrian, we learn how vulnerable Rome is to enemy assault now that Coriolanus has been driven out.

Immediately afterward we see Coriolanus *"in mean apparel, disguis'd and muffled"* before the house of his arch-enemy, Aufidius. Where has he been up until now and why has he come here? These questions are left suspended while Coriolanus delivers a cryptic soliloquy. His momentous decision to turn traitor to Rome and join with his enemy is made to depend upon the caprice of Fortune, "Some trick not worth an egg" (4.4.21), and the theme of the soliloquy is: "O world, thy slippery turns!" (12). In the next scene, he boldly presents himself to Aufidius during a feast and joins forces with him. By a subtle collocation of scenes, Shakespeare has dropped hints that he doesn't wish to develop, so that we may move quickly and without transition from Coriolanus in Rome to Coriolanus in Antium. Abrupt contrast is a more characteristically Shakespearean device than logical progression.

In *The Winter's Tale*, the necessary psychological explanations for Leontes's jealousy are also suppressed. It comes upon him like a fit of madness, and it is already at its peak in his first aside, as the hypnotic doubling of his words seems to indicate:

> Too hot, too hot!
> To mingle friendship far is mingling bloods.
> I have tremor cordis on me; my heart dances,
> But not for joy, not joy.
>
> (1.2.108–11)

This is very different from the slowly articulated jealousy of Othello, on whom Leontes is modeled. Unlike Othello, Leontes seems to grow more lyrical as his jealous fit overpowers his reason; his strong emotions make for a corresponding intensity in the poetry. Leontes abandons his jealousy with the same swiftness he first indulged it. He is not ready to believe the truth of Apollo's oracle until a servant enters to announce the death of the King's son. Then Leontes suddenly realizes his folly, and his jealous fit is over: "Apollo's angry; and the heavens themselves/ Do strike at my injustice" (3.2.143–44). No effort is made to explain his change of heart. The powerful recognition speech we expect from Shakespearean tragedy would be inappropriate here, because Leontes is not the sort of character whose inner life is revealed to the audience.

Sudden repentances at death are more or less the expected norm in Shakespeare, and they demonstrate how moral conventions may impose their own pattern on the developing sequence of events. The mere presence of the executioner seems to inspire thoughts of justice and salvation. "Nothing in his life/ Became him like the leaving it," says Malcolm of the traitor Cawdor (*Macbeth* 1.4.7–8). Before he died,

> very frankly he confess'd his treasons,
> Implor'd your Highness' pardon, and set
> forth
> A deep repentance.
>
> (1.4.5–7)

This provides what is almost a formula for traitors' deaths, no matter how dastardly their previous career has been.

The history plays are full of these conventionally remorseful death speeches. With explicit, rhetorical amplification, the conspirators in *Henry* V express their guilt for what they have done. Lord Scroop declares: "Our purposes God justly hath discover'd,/ And I repent my fault more than my death" (2.2.151–52). The Earl of Cambridge thanks God "for prevention" (158), and Sir Thomas Grey, the last in the formal procession, is almost overwhelmed by his own ecstatic self-condemnation:

> Never did faithful subject more rejoice
> At the discovery of most dangerous treason
> Than I do at this hour joy o'er myself,
> Prevented from a damned enterprise.
> My fault, but not my body, pardon,
> sovereign.
>
> (2.2.161–65)

This is the great moment for Scroop, Cambridge, and Grey, who, apart from their deaths, have no interest at all as characters. Their speeches are intended to celebrate both God's inscrutable wisdom and Henry V's astute management of the realm.

We are willing to accept gaps in the presentation of Shakespeare's characters, quick changes in their development, and other moral conventions, because we are not committed to seeing them as real people. Once we firmly believe that they are imaginative constructs, then anything is possible. Shakespeare sometimes violates the common sense of our expectations, even seems to play tricks on us. I am thinking particularly of Richard II, who begins the play as a weak, ceremonial king and gradually deteriorates to a cruel, capricious, frivolous tyrant. His lowest point in our esteem is the scene with the dying Gaunt, whom Richard reviles as "A lunatic lean-witted fool,/ Presuming on an ague's privilege" (2.1.115–16). Once Gaunt is dead, Richard seizes his estate, although Bolingbroke, his son and heir, is alive. This arbitrary act precipitates Richard's fall, when Bolingbroke returns to England to claim his own.

Richard is quickly thrust into adversity, and as soon as it is apparent that Bolingbroke will become king, we begin to pity Richard in his misfortune. We forget his failures and concentrate on his suffering. We suddenly discover a religious turn in the imagery; Richard mocks all royal pomp, which he will gladly exchange for monastic simplicity:

> I'll give my jewels for a set of beads,
> My gorgeous palace for a hermitage,
> My gay apparel for an almsman's gown,
> My figur'd goblets for a dish of wood,
> My sceptre for a palmer's walking staff,
> My subjects for a pair of carved saints,
> And my large kingdom for a little grave,
> A little little grave, an obscure grave....
>
> (3.3.147–54)

The poetic style is mannered, if not affected, and Richard pursues conceits to absurd limits, yet he powerfully elicits our pity for what is happening to him. We do not wince even when, in the deposition scene, he freely compares himself to Christ:

> Nay, all of you that stand and look upon me
> Whilst that my wretchedness doth bait
> myself,

> Though some of you, with Pilate, wash your
> hands,
> Showing an outward pity—yet you Pilates
> Have here deliver'd me to my sour cross,
> And water cannot wash away your sin.
> (4.1.237–42)

The Richard of the beginning of the play has been forgotten, and in his agony and death he achieves tragic stature. From the music he hears in his prison, he comes to an insight like that of King Lear: "For 'tis a sign of love; and love to Richard/ Is a strange brooch in this all-hating world" (5.5.65–66).

Shakespeare's characters sometimes speak not for themselves but for the play.

❮ Critics have taken Shakespeare's characters to task for being "out of character." But what does being "in character" mean? The need for dramatic persons to be consistent throughout their plays—as if the plays were slices of life—may be foreign to Shakespeare's art. Many speeches are the product of the occasion rather than the personal mood of the speaker, and any attempt to tie the speaker closely to his words may lead to dead ends, where the character is speaking not in his own behalf, but for the benefit of the play.

There is a teasing example in *The Tempest* of the seeming autonomy of style apart from character. The plot against Prospero has a savagery not unexpected from someone as servile and depraved as Caliban:

> Why, as I told thee, 'tis a custom with him
> [= Prospero]
> I' th' afternoon to sleep; there thou mayst
> brain him,
> Having first seiz'd his books; or with a log
> Batter his skull, or paunch him with a stake,
> Or cut his wezand with thy knife.
> (3.2.83–87)

This crude and uninventive violence is "in character," but not long after, in answer to Ariel's mocking tabor and pipe, Caliban delivers what is perhaps the most lyric speech in the play:

> Be not afeard. The isle is full of noises,
> Sounds, and sweet airs, that give delight,
>   and hurt not.
> Sometimes a thousand twangling instru-
>   ments
> Will hum about mine ears; and sometime
>   voices,
> That, if I then had wak'd after long sleep,
> Will make me sleep again; and then, in
>   dreaming,
> The clouds methought would open and
>   show riches
> Ready to drop upon me, that, when I wak'd,
> I cried to dream again.
>
> (3.2.130–38)

What is the connection between this speech and the previous one, where Caliban is ready to "paunch" Prospero "with a stake,/ Or cut his wezand" with a knife?

Merely to ask the question assumes that there is an answer, but the tone of these two speeches cannot be reconciled by the subtleties of character analysis. "The isle is full of noises" does not reveal a hidden aspect of Caliban, but rather makes him contribute, almost involuntarily, to the sense of wonder in the play. He celebrates the beauty and mystery of nature not because he is of a religious turn, nor a natural child of the island, but because he is a character in *The Tempest*. Caliban's speech has no preparation and no follow-up, and it is all the more extraordinary in its drunken, conspiratorial, low-comedy context. Even if it seems to us "out of character" for Caliban, it is completely in keeping with the spirit of the play.

The loose relation of speaker to speech may be demonstrated most tellingly in Shakespeare's death speeches. Praise of the dead is expected regardless of what the immediate situation has been, and the speaker of the eulogy is often not at all the one best qualified to memorialize a departed friend. Why should Antony be singled out in *Julius Caesar* to tell us that Brutus "was the noblest Roman of them all" (5.5.68)? There is nothing in the relationship of Antony and Brutus that would make him a logical choice for Brutus's eulogizer, so that we are forced to look at this death speech apart from the character of Antony. The virtues he extols in the dead Brutus are not at all those he admires in the play. He is certainly no lover either of Brutus's "general honest thought/ And common good to all" (5.5.71–72) or of his well-tempered disposition:

> the elements
> So mix'd in him that Nature might stand up
> And say to all the world 'This was a man!'
> (5.5.73–75)

We are not, of course, meant to think that Antony is a hypocrite to speak this way; he is fulfilling the rhetorical demands of the occasion without involving himself in character implications.

In *Antony and Cleopatra*, the death of Antony seems to elicit a fund of compassion in Octavius Caesar, his rival, that is matched nowhere else in the play. This would be a remarkable discovery about the character of Caesar, if it were indeed about Caesar rather than about Antony. Caesar's first reaction to Antony's death is full of generosity and poetic magnitude:

> The breaking of so great a thing should
>   make
> A greater crack. The round world
> Should have shook lions into civil streets,
> And citizens to their dens. The death of
>   Antony
> Is not a single doom: in the name lay
> A moiety of the world.
> (5.1.14–19)

A "moiety" is half, but Caesar knows that he is the greater half. In his next speech, Caesar seems either to be weeping or on the point of tears:

> Look you sad, friends?
> The gods rebuke me, but it is tidings
> To wash the eyes of kings.
>
> (5.1.26–28)

Further on, Caesar is lamenting "With tears as sovereign as the blood of hearts" (41). These speeches, however, are the last we hear of Caesar's grief for Antony.

In *Hamlet*, Gertrude narrates with lyric circumstantiality Ophelia's death by water. She begins by setting the pastoral scene: "There is a willow grows aslant the brook/ That shows his hoar leaves in the glassy stream . . ." (4.7. 167–68). Gertrude has never spoken so musically anywhere else in the play, but her sudden gift is a tribute to Ophelia—and like Ophelia's style—rather than the revelation of a hidden aspect of the Queen. With a mixture of passionate exactness and figurative adornment, Gertrude continues her description of Ophelia's death:

> Her clothes spread wide
> And, mermaid-like, awhile they bore her up;
> Which time she chanted snatches of old
>   lauds,
> As one incapable of her own distress,
> Or like a creature native and indued
> Unto that element; but long it could not be
> Till that her garments, heavy with their
>   drink,
> Pull'd the poor wretch from her melodious
>   lay
> To muddy death.
>
> (4.7.176–84)

The beauty of the verse celebrates the beauty of Ophelia. Is this speech "out of character" for Gertrude? In order to put it "in character," we would have to ask why she just stood there watching and didn't rush in to save the drowning girl. It is a tribute to Shakespeare's dramatic power that this question never occurs to audiences of *Hamlet*, who are perfectly willing to suspend their disbelief and listen to Gertrude's speech without making any intrusive character demands.

There is probably much less dialogue and many more set speeches in Shakespeare's plays than is generally thought. This doesn't make the plays less dramatic, but only more formal and more frankly rhetorical. The set speeches are used for narrations, anticipations, soliloquies, orations, special pleadings, and many other explanatory and emotive purposes. Shakespeare's audience is ready to listen to long declamations without feeling that the action of the play has stopped or that the playwright is violating his commitment to dialogue. While the speech is being delivered, we are obliged to suspend many of our strict demands for "in-character" relevance.

In the death speeches discussed above, there was a potential clash between the role that seemed to be created by the speech and the characterization in the rest of the play. This ambiguity of reference applies generally to all set speeches. Everything depends on whether the audience will put the emphasis on the speaker or on the speech. Enobarbus's magnificent description of Cleopatra in her barge on the Cydnus is a case in point. It is significant that Enobarbus rather than Antony should celebrate Cleopatra's attraction, since Antony never speaks rapturously about her at all—she is too much of a mystery to him.

It is difficult, however, to go further and connect this panegyric with the character of Enobarbus, who is usually a blunt, witty speaker like Kent in *Lear*. The delicate, hyperbolical, mythological imagery is not in Enobarbus's expected style:

> She did lie
> In her pavilion, cloth-of-gold, of tissue,
> O'erpicturing that Venus where we see
> The fancy out-work nature. On each side her
> Stood pretty dimpled boys, like smiling
>   Cupids,
> With divers-colour'd fans, whose wind did
>   seem
> To glow the delicate cheeks which they did
>   cool,
> And what they undid did.
>   (2.2.202–9)

The aesthetic stasis of "what they undid did" is not calculated to appeal to a rough campaigner like Enobarbus, nor are the "pretty dimpled boys" who set the air in motion with their "divers-colour'd fans." Enobarbus means to impress his listeners, the Roman soldiers Maecenas and Agrippa, and he delivers his account of Cleopatra with rhetorical gusto, but he is not so much speaking for himself as for the play. We are meant to enjoy his speech without trying to integrate it into the dramatic character of the speaker.

It seems to me that Shakespeare's characters rarely give the impression that they are independent beings, who, once set in motion, are free to work out their own destiny. On the contrary, they are tightly controlled by the author, and there are moments in all of the plays when the demands of the play override those of the characters. I don't mean to raise the issue, from Aristotle's *Poetics*, about the relative superiority of the dramatic action to the characters, but Shakespeare does seem to put the needs of his subject, theme, or plot before those of his dramatic persons. There is no conflict here, only a question of priorities. By developing his characters with so much deliberate skill, Shakespeare abandons any claim that they are natural energies captured by the playwright within his dramatic medium. The characters are not "natural" at all, but a product of their creator's imaginative art.

Structure and Dramatic Scene

*The Shakespearean scene is
defined by the confrontation of
persons rather than
by geographical place.*

❨ Any discussion of Shakespeare's scenes depends on what
we know about the Elizabethan theater and its possibilities. Very little was done on the Elizabethan stage to
create the illusion of place. Painted, movable scenery was
not in general use until the end of the seventeenth century, so that our understanding of "scene" as a location
does not hold for Elizabethan drama. On the modern
realistic stage, and especially in the movies, a change of
scene means a change of place; but if no places are
strongly delineated, then our whole notion of scene as a
change of place needs to be reexamined. In Elizabethan
drama the separate scenes are defined by the characters
in them and the significant encounters of those characters,
rather than by the places in which the action is imagined
to occur.

This distinction is an important first premise for understanding Elizabethan dramaturgy. It is possible in Shakespeare to have scenes that are set in no place more
specific than the stage itself. The battle scenes in the last
act of *Henry IV, Part 1,* for example, are essentially un-
located. In Alexander's edition, which follows the traditional scene indications of Shakespeare's eighteenth-
century editors, Act V, scene i, is fixed in *"The King's*

camp near Shrewsbury." But in the early quarto and folio texts there is no mention at all of Shrewsbury, although there may have been some tents on stage to suggest a military encampment. We are told elsewhere that this scene takes place near Shrewsbury, and the location is also a matter of historical record, but from the audience's point of view the military parley might be occurring anywhere in England. Alexander puts Act V, scene ii, in "*The rebel camp*," which doesn't strain our credulity, but Act V, scene iii, in "A *plain between the camps*" makes demands on our localization far in excess of what the Elizabethan stage could offer. There is nothing in the scene of a "*plain*" —this is the sort of topography movies can render well, as in Olivier's celebrated version of *Henry V*—nor is "*between the camps*" anything except an intellectual formulation.

Act V, scene iv, has that classic direction: "*Another part of the field.*" How, logically, can this be "*Another part of the field*" if we were never convinced that the stage was a field at all? We are in "*Another part of the field*" because we have a different set of characters from the previous scene and not because of any change in location. I have no objection to scene headings that may help us visualize the action on the modern stage, but it should be made apparent that they have nothing at all to do with Elizabethan staging.

Without the encumbrance of located places, Shakespeare's scenes can move easily into each other in an uninterrupted sequence. There is no time out for changing scenes, and the few properties needed might either be brought on by the characters or thrust on stage from behind. In this way, Shakespeare's plays maintain a pace almost unimaginable in a modern production. The prologue to *Romeo and Juliet* speaks of "the two hours' traffic of our stage," which is a limit often mentioned in other plays. Admittedly, two hours is a round number, but even if two and a half hours are meant, this would still be a remarkably swift *Romeo and Juliet*. There is no inherent advantage in finishing the play in such a short time, except that the dramatic effect can be intensified. We should not diffuse the hard-won attention of the audience or distract them from the feeling of climax. Thus, a tragedy can have a more concentrated impact, and even in the more leisurely world of comedy, the complications can multiply without any loss of momentum.

One of the advantages of looking at structure in terms of scenes is that it forces us to found our argument on what actually happens in the play rather than on theoretical dispositions. The scenes reveal an empirical structure that may be different from what we create in our analytic models. The notion of context is also important here. Each scene occurs in relation to other scenes, and the development, complication, or intensification in the middle of plays depends upon context for its effect. A certain kind of scene toward the end of a play is different from the same kind of scene very early in the action. The audience thinks naturally in comparisons, and it develops its own scale of structural relevance while watching the play. From the pattern of contrasted and seemingly fragmentary scenes, we should pick up hints that will later be developed, and we should be able to sharpen our sensitivity to what is about to happen.

The scene is the basic structural unit in Shakespeare and the action progresses by scenic contrast.

In studying Shakespeare's dramatic art, we keep coming back to Hamlet's notion of the "very cunning of the scene" (2.2.586). The action does not move in a straight line from beginning to end, but rather sideways, as one group of characters and one sequence of scenes are set against another. Different lines are developed simultaneously and are made to comment on each other by analogy. This is most apparent in plays with a multiple plot, such as *King Lear*, where the Lear and the Gloucester actions are mutually illuminating. But even where there are no separate plots, the effect of analogy is still strong. Thus, Hamlet, Laertes, and Fortinbras are all pursuing the same ends for similar reasons.

Scenic contrast in Elizabethan drama is like montage in the movies. Both present a mosaic of small pieces of action set side by side, which relate to each other by the mere fact of propinquity. Montage also uses quick, bold contrasts without any transition, so that the spectator is forced to establish connections for himself. I don't mean to imply that the movies borrow Elizabethan techniques, but the dramatic construction in the movies and in Shakespeare is more consciously an artifice than that in realistic plays, and it expects the audience to be aware of the illusion.

In *Antony and Cleopatra*, for example, the symbolic contrast between Egypt and Rome governs the scenic contrast in the play, according to the simple principle of alternation. The scenes may be very short, sometimes shorter than fifty lines, but they are played off against each other in rapid sequence. The overlapping in time of successive scenes does not in any way affect the forward movement of the action. In Act I, scene iv, for example, Caesar is hoping that Antony will leave his "lascivious wassails" (56) in Egypt at the very moment we know that he has already left them. Similarly, Pompey in Act II, scene i, wishes that Cleopatra will continue to "Tie up the libertine in a field of feasts" (23), just before Varrius enters to announce that Antony is expected shortly in Rome. The two sides of the alternating scenes remain independent but interrelated; they are not simply building blocks piled one on top of the other.

A sequence of alternating scenes in Act III shows us the rivalry between Cleopatra and Octavia for the possession of Antony, but the underlying issue is the conflict between Antony and Caesar. In these five short scenes (3.2–6), none more than a hundred lines, this conflict is quickly developed into open war. By using five short scenes, Shakespeare can skip over intermediate stages and thereby tighten his presentation. He can also develop the action in terms of different characters, which helps to create a composite, multiple sense of what is happening. By not limiting the point of view, he can swing back and forth to both sides of a divided action.

Despite the preoccupation of critics with the love affair of Antony and Cleopatra, military scenes dominate the play. There are three distinct battle sequences in Acts III and IV. The first is that of Actium, which begins in Act III, scene vii, with the strongest possible tokens of Antony's inevitable defeat. He indulges Cleopatra's petulant desire to appear "for a man" (18), and he gives way to his own chivalric impulse to fight Caesar at sea, even though it is against both good sense and good strategy. The next two scenes have only six and four lines, as we catch a glimpse of Caesar at one side of the stage and Antony at the other. Their tactics are demonstrated in the dumb show that opens Act III, scene x: "CANIDIUS *marcheth with his land Army one way over the stage, and* TAURUS, *the Lieutenant of Caesar, the other way.*" In the midst of these military maneuvers that have nothing directly to do with the battle of Actium, we hear *"the noise of a sea-fight"* off-stage. By the time Enobarbus enters to speak the first line of this scene—"Naught, naught, all naught! I can behold no longer" (3.10.1)—the battle is already over, and we learn about it retrospectively through the conversation of Antony's soldiers.

In the third battle sequence, two very brief scenes of nine and four lines—Act IV, scenes x and xi—reveal the intentions of Antony and Caesar, and the battle occurs swiftly in scene xii. The *"Alarum afar off, as at a sea-fight"* reminds us of the battle of Actium, where we learn what has happened only through the account of witnesses. The general rule in Shakespearean staging is that, although we may see their periphery, the battles themselves take place off-stage.

The battle sequences in *Antony and Cleopatra* are characteristic of Shakespeare's presentation of momentous events: they are always panoramic and symbolic rather than realistic. An actual naval battle is outside the possibilities of the Elizabethan stage, but even land battles are presented indirectly by brief encounters and little vignettes of action. The scenic contrasts show the battle as a composite of significant pieces. There is no way on the Elizabethan stage to show us the direct encounter of masses of men, as Eisenstein does so convincingly in the movie *Alexander Nevsky*. Shakespeare stays within the scenic limitations of his theater, but he also makes a virtue of these limitations. If his battle scenes lack grandeur, they profit from being conceived on the human scale, with conflicts between distinct individuals on either side.

Choral scenes in *Antony and Cleopatra* have an entirely different structural purpose from the scenes of battle. They offer a significant way of commenting on the action without involving any of the major characters. Shakespeare uses these kinds of scenes to accomplish some of the functions of the chorus in classical drama, and they provide a freer, more poetic, and more philosophical discourse than is possible in ordinary dialogue. The choral scenes are unexpected, and the persons in them are usually minor, anonymous, or type characters, who have no further role in the play.

Antony and Cleopatra opens with a scene that is choral in intent, as Philo, a soldier in Antony's army, explains to his companion, Demetrius, the "dotage" Cleopatra has wrought in Antony:

> His captain's heart,
> Which in the scuffles of great fights hath
>   burst
> The buckles on his breast, reneges all temper,
> And is become the bellows and the fan
> To cool a gipsy's lust.
>
> (1.1.6–10)

These judgments establish a strong attitude to Antony—and also to Cleopatra. In its simple and bold moralism, Philo's speech seems an odd way to begin this most morally ambiguous of Shakespeare's plays, but it does offer a clear formulation by which to test the scenes that will follow. In another moment, we see "The triple pillar of the world transform'd/ Into a strumpet's fool" (12–13), as Antony enters with Cleopatra, *"her Ladies, the Train, with Eunuchs fanning her."* Philo and Demetrius stand aside, but everything we see and hear confirms their harsh, Roman view of Antony. By delivering the opening and closing comments in this scene, they function as presenters of the action.

Any two scenes that are juxtaposed will seem to have some relation to each other, so that the dramatist may choose to make the second scene a choral undercutting of the first. The sequence of Pompey scenes, for example, ends with a splendid party aboard Pompey's galley to celebrate his peace with the triumvirs (2.7). It is the only merry scene in the play, as the "three world-sharers," Antony, Caesar, and Lepidus, dance and sing in drunken revelry. Pompey's officer, Menas, has a wonderfully simple plan to set the galley adrift, cut the triumvirs' throats, and make Pompey lord of all the world, but Pompey would like to profit from this scheme without actually participating in it.

A disquieting choral scene follows immediately after Act II, scene vii. Ventidius, a commander of Antony's army, patiently explains to Silius why he will not pursue his Parthian conquest:

> Who does i' th' wars more than his captain
>   can
> Becomes his captain's captain; and ambition,
> The soldier's virtue, rather makes choice of
>   loss
> Than gain which darkens him.
> I could do more to do Antonius good,
> But 'twould offend him; and in his offense
> Should my performance perish.
>
>   (3.1.21–27)

The fullness of reasoning is unexpected. The Parthian campaign has no direct relation to the main action, yet Ventidius's reluctance suggests something corrupt in Antony's military hierarchy. All is not so merry as it seemed in the previous scene, particularly with Antony. Ventidius and Menas have a good deal in common, although Menas learns painfully in Act II, scene vii, what Ventidius already knows full well in Act III, scene i. Pompey and Antony also have much in common, and the speeches of Menas and Ventidius mark the falls of their respective leaders. By making the brief scene of Ventidius the beginning of Act III, Shakespeare's editors have badly distracted us from its natural pairing with the last scene of Act II.

The fall of Antony is also projected in the choral scene of Act IV, scene iii. From the conversation of the soldiers on the night before the second battle, we feel a sense of foreboding doom. They place themselves symbolically *"in every corner of the stage,"* and we suddenly hear the strange music of hautboys, or oboes, from *"under the stage."* "It signs well, does it not?" asks the Fifth Soldier tentatively, but no, it is an evil sign, as the Second Soldier explains: " 'Tis the god Hercules, whom Antony lov'd,/ Now leaves him" (16–17). Hercules was Antony's tutelary deity, and his departure seals the fate of Antony, despite his deceptive victory in the next day's battle. Enobarbus also leaves Antony at about this time. Act IV, scene iii, is set among battle scenes, but it is entirely different from the dialogue of familiar characters in the scenes that precede and follow. The unnamed soldiers of Act IV, scene iii, represent the sort of collective insight that one finds in the Greek chorus, and their comments expand the dimension of the action. As in plays with oracles and supernatural forces, especially *Macbeth*, we are meant to see the drama acting out the will of the gods.

I have considered only three kinds of scenes in *Antony and Cleopatra*, a play in which the scenic art is as complex as it is anywhere in Shakespeare. It is not the forty-two scenes that make it complex, but the "infinite variety" of their disposition. They fall into coherent sequences that define the structure of the play, which does not correspond to the conventional division into five acts. We have already noticed the close connection between Act II, scene vii, and Act III, scene i. There is a similar link between Act III, scene xiii, and Act IV, scene i; the later scene continues the earlier one, as we see Caesar scorning Antony's desperate challenge to single combat. The modern five acts of *Antony and Cleopatra* seem to have no theatrical significance, but the forty-two scenes reveal most artfully the play's analogical method of construction.

Many of Shakespeare's plays in the Folio of 1623 have some indications of acts (although not usually all the way through), but there is good reason to doubt whether Shakespeare marked them that way. Most of the act divisions are the product of later editors, who were trying to make Shakespeare a more classically "regular" dramatist by dignifying his plays with a five-act structure. *Henry* V and *Pericles* are clearly five-act plays, with each unit introduced by a choral prologue, but these are exceptions, and most of Shakespeare's plays do not have this pentagonal symmetry. In a modern production, it would be inconceivable to adhere strictly to the five-act scheme. Not only would four prominent breaks in the action seem tedious and unnecessary, but they would also disturb the swift continuity that is such an important feature of Elizabethan staging.

Shakespeare's plays have district beginnings, middles and ends.

❪ In the theater the basic quality of structure is extension or duration; plays exist only in the dimension of time, most obviously the time of performance. If all plays must have a beginning, middle, and end, as Aristotle specified in his *Poetics*, then the parts of the action relate to each other by their position in the time sequence. A presented play moves with an inevitability different from a play on the printed page, where we can stop at any point and even return to a previous section according to our own sense of what is important. The strict temporal limits of a play force it to be simpler and more emphatic in structure than other literary forms. This is true even for Shakespeare—perhaps especially for Shakespeare—whose plays are articulated with unusual clarity and lucidity. Not that Shakespeare is not also complex, but his complexities appear as if superimposed on his simplicities.

The beginnings of Shakespeare's plays confirm the explicitness of his structure. Not just information is communicated to the audience, but attitudes, character implications, suggestions of theme, and many other necessary clues for understanding the play. The audience presumably starts from point zero. First impressions are of crucial importance not only because they fill a void, but also because they establish patterns of expectation for all else that is to follow. We try to reason from the opening parts to the whole. The playwright may be deliberately leading us astray, but this is a moment of great receptivity, when we are trying to fathom what the play is about, whether we like it, and perhaps also whether we will immediately leave the theater. Shakespeare's beginnings are conceived in terms of the potential responses of the audience, and this first contact between audience and play is an exciting moment.

The middles of plays are much less clearly defined than the beginnings and ends. Once the same characters reappear, we know that the primary exposition is over. The emphasis shifts from learning about the history and background of the characters to observing them in their immediate situation. This part of the play is variously called the epitasis, the complication, the "thickening"—as if the plot were a soup (*la bonne soupe*) that thickens as it boils. If we take "denouement" literally as a structural term, then "knotting" is a useful metaphor for this part of the play, in which the various strands of the action are deliberately knotted up so that the playwright may have the pleasure of unknotting them in the end. (I recognize that the terms I have been using are more relevant to comedy than to tragedy, since comedy puts more emphasis on the plot mechanism, and it uses structural devices more freely and self-consciously than does tragedy.)

As the dramatic action is complicated and intensified in

the middle of the play, it reaches a crisis point beyond which it cannot be developed any further. This begins the resolution, when knots will be untied, difficulties cleared up, and the plot set right for the audience. In comedy everything moves toward a "happy" ending, with weddings, feasting, revelry, dancing, and song, whereas in tragedy everything moves toward the deaths of the protagonist, the antagonist, and many of those allied with them. The evil which generated the action is destroyed, expelled, nullified, or converted to good, but only at a terrible price. Tragedies usually end with the suggestion of a new order, but the outlook is not optimistic, because we feel that this new order is of a lesser magnitude than that originally promised by the protagonist.

Shakespeare's beginnings, middles, and ends represent his dramatic structure in terms of movement, development, progression, unfolding—what has been called the tragic or comic rhythm. In other words, a certain kind of beginning implies a compatible middle and end, or the emphasis might fall on a powerful end to which everything has been inevitably leading. Drama as a form sets up expectations that it must try to fulfill, or, to turn the perspective around, it projects fulfillments that must have an adequate pattern of expectations. In any case, Aristotle's three conditions should be taken together as a single, imaginative whole. There is an implicit assumption that human experience, which supplies the plots for plays, also has beginnings, middles, and ends, and is causative, rational, progressive, and triadic in structure.

The beginnings, middles, and ends of Shakespeare's comedies.

❲ The most familiar opening in comedy is the outrageous edict or proposition, which creates an extreme situation that must be resolved. In *The Comedy of Errors*, it just so happens that Aegeon, the merchant of Syracuse, is going to be put to death by the law of Ephesus that condemns all Syracusans who cannot pay a ransom of a thousand marks. Aegeon's doom is suspended over the play and never completely forgotten while we occupy ourselves with other matters. No real effort is ever made to justify this law or even to protest against it. It is accepted as an arbitrary decree of Fortune, and the more capricious and unreasonable it is, the more dazzling will be the playwright's skill in extricating his personages.

This kind of beginning has a strong thrust to it, so that we immediately want to know how it will turn out. Our curiosity is piqued and our interest is engaged. In *A Midsummer Night's Dream,* Egeus, the "heavy" father, invokes an "ancient privilege of Athens" (1.1.41) to force his daughter Hermia either to marry Demetrius or to die. She, of course, with the full approval of the audience, decides to run away, and thus the mistakes of the lovers in a wood near Athens develop from the first step of the outrageous edict. *Measure for Measure* also generates its action by the revival of a disused law that makes fornication punishable by death.

The catalyst for the action need not necessarily be a law. Any extreme proposition will do, even that the suitor to the youngest daughter must first provide a husband for the eldest, which is only extreme when the eldest daughter is as cursed, forward, and refractory as Katherine in *The Taming of the Shrew.* In *Love's Labour's Lost,* we begin with a proposal that flagrantly violates common sense and normal expectations. The King of Navarre has converted his court into a Platonic Academy, and his three disciples have vowed, for a three-year term, to see no women, to follow a monastic rule, and to devote their manly energies to study. Will they be able to keep their vows? Even in the first scene, Berowne is already introducing disruptive possibilities:

> Necessity will make us all forsworn
> Three thousand times within this three
>   years' space;

> For every man with his affects is born,
> Not by might mast'red, but by special grace.
>
> (1.1.147–50)

A play that begins with a strange and unusual edict or an outrageous proposition demands a structure that will nullify and revoke the original statement. We know at once that the first formulation cannot hold, but the ingenuity with which it will be undone proves the comic skill of the playwright.

If, as Lysander informs us, "The course of true love never did run smooth" (A *Midsummer Night's Dream* 1.1.134), then the difficulties of lovers fill the middles of most comedies. There is an apt example of love complications in *The Tempest,* a play that has more to tell us about pedagogy than any other of Shakespeare's works —and Prospero the magician is Shakespeare's prime example of the teacher. Although Prospero wishes to bring Ferdinand and Miranda together and seems to shipwreck the Tunisian wedding guests for this very purpose, he also sets obstacles in their path. Prospero is churlish to Ferdinand, accuses him of being a spy, and takes him prisoner—all in order to arouse Miranda's tender sympathies. For the old-fashioned Prospero, love at first sight is not an adequate basis for marriage, as he explains to us in an aside:

> They are both in either's pow'rs; but this
>   swift business
> I must uneasy make, lest too light winning
> Make the prize light.
>
> (1.2.450–52)

Would that Friar Lawrence in *Romeo and Juliet* had acted on the same principle!

At the beginning of Act III, scene i, we see Ferdinand *"bearing a log,"* as in the previous scene Caliban entered *"with a burden of wood."* Unlike Caliban, however, Ferdinand is a "patient log-man" (3.1.67), who separates his noble nature from the base tasks that have been imposed on him. As he tells us in the soliloquy that opens this scene:

> some kinds of baseness
> Are nobly undergone, and most poor matters
> Point to rich ends. This my mean task
> Would be as heavy to me as odious, but
> The mistress which I serve quickens what's
>   dead,
> And makes my labours pleasures.
>
> (3.1.2–7)

He sees at once that his labor is a love trial and wisely refuses Miranda's proffered help. He continues to haul logs throughout this scene, but his forced labor is soon forgotten in the passionate enthusiasm of the love talk.

The difficulties that beset lovers in Shakespeare's comedies all seem artificial when taken out of context, because love itself and its conventions are so artificial. Love at first sight is assumed, which always puts the lovers in the perilous position of being able to fall in love with someone else with equal facility. Emotions are highly stylized, so that one may be rapturously in love or desolately out of love by a few accepted rhetorical devices or by a few easily recognized changes in one's appearance. In *A Midsummer Night's Dream*, Shakespeare seems to ridicule love conventions by using love juice to mix up the lovers. Does Puck delight in complications or does he make genuine errors? It really doesn't matter, because Puck's mischief generates our delight in the play, as Lysander and Demetrius both pursue Helena, and Hermia pursues the now scornful Lysander. Puck finally sets all to rights, and we have the impression that the lovers profit from their strange experiences in the wood. The thickening of the plot has all the animated and frenzied activity of a dream; once the lovers return to their Athenian setting, we lose interest in their everyday, domestic reality.

The most frequent way of complicating comedies is to introduce an element of comic villainy, which we may define broadly as any kind of plot directed against a character. It is usually intended to expose eccentric and socially unacceptable behavior. By putting the ridiculous person out of his humor, it becomes possible for him to reenter the normal, healthy, witty world of the play. Petruchio's taming of his shrewish wife plainly demonstrates the use of comic villainy for a didactic purpose. Petruchio is cruel, harsh, impolite, sardonic, barbarous, and tyrannical to his Kate, but all in a good cause. His success is attested by his disciple, Hortensio, who comes to Petruchio's "taming school" to learn how to manage his own widow.

In Shakespeare's more complex comedies, there is usually at least one figure who defies all attempts to integrate him into the world of the play. In *Twelfth Night*, the plot against Malvolio fails in its ultimate objective to humanize him and teach him the ways of the world. The plotters are confirmed in their own social values without being able to convert Malvolio, who is exposed to laughing scorn but not reformed. This practical joke—villainy from Malvolio's point of view—defines the structure of the middle of the play. Like Malvolio, Shylock is also "a kind of Puritan" (*Twelfth Night* 2.3.131), and he too is untouched by the plots against him. He may be forcibly converted to Christianity at the end, but he cannot be converted to the Christian ethics of Portia's appeal. And in *As You Like It*, the malcontent Jaques will not abandon the Forest of Arden for the civilized pleasures and responsibilities of Duke Senior's court.

Comedies are generally ended by the conventional assumption that all previous difficulties were merely an illusion. In *The Comedy of Errors*, for example, the impending death of Aegeon is about to take place when he is recognized as the long-lost husband of the Abbess and the father of the Antipholus twins. The recognitions create a new mood as the once shipwrecked family are restored to each other. We have a sense of unbounded acceleration in these final events, so that there is no possible proportion between the elaborate development of the middle and the speedy resolution of the end. In

Twelfth Night, the twins are sorted out, all disguises are removed, all perturbations are quieted, all marriages are made after the fondest wishes of the parties, and everyone except Malvolio joins in the fun. There is a feeling not only of clarification at the end of these comedies, but also of luminousness. Even in *Measure for Measure*, which begins darkly, the ending celebrates forgiveness, forbearance, and mercy, which are erected into a legal principle that can challenge the Old Testament *lex talionis*, an eye for an eye. The comic spirit of these conclusions is best described in the final couplet of *All's Well That Ends Well*:

> All yet seems well; and if it end so meet,
> The bitter past, more welcome is the sweet.
>
> (5.3.326–27)

The endings of Shakespeare's last romances exploit wonders and marvels, which develop out of the tragicomic complications that have preceded. The resurrection of Hermione in *The Winter's Tale* is performed with religious and aesthetic ceremony in Paulina's chapel. From a statue cunningly carved by Julio Romano, Hermione is returned to life—to her husband and to her newly found daughter. Why has it taken Paulina sixteen years to restore the supposedly dead Hermione? The question remains unanswered, but Paulina's show is perfect in all its details, and it represents at its best the beautiful artifice of these late plays. Leontes, who is "mock'd with art" (5.3.68), presses passionately to verify his aesthetic experience:

> Still, methinks,
> There is an air comes from her. What fine
>   chisel
> Could ever yet cut breath? Let no man mock
>   me,
> For I will kiss her.
>
> (5.3.77–80)

Paulina tries conscientiously to prolong the illusion:

> Good my lord, forbear.
> The ruddiness upon her lip is wet;

> You'll mar it if you kiss it; stain your own
> With oily painting. Shall I draw the curtain?
> (5.3.80–83)

In some metaphoric sense, Hermione's sixteen-year absence has made her into a work of art for Leontes, but art and reality are deliberately confounded.

The beginnings, middles, and ends of Shakespeare's tragedies.

❴ If evil is the special concern of tragedy, there is a striking difference between the beginnings of comedies and tragedies. A Shakespearean comedy may be generated by an outrageous edict or proposition, but the action remains arbitrary and capricious, detached and independent of any significant context. In tragedy, however, the emphasis falls on the consequences of willful, petulant, unjust, or tyrannical acts. King Lear is not allowed the self-indulgence that his rejection of Cordelia might provoke in comedy. He is almost at once plunged into perturbation and chaos, both personal and political, and the storm carries the metaphor of discord into the very nature of things. Whatever the comic potentialities of the plot, the beginnings of Shakespeare's tragedies move swiftly into symbolic projections of evil. The feuding houses in *Romeo and Juliet* are at first amusing in their preoccupation with tokens, words, and identifying marks, but the deadly hate soon shows itself and poisons all. Something is indeed rotten in the state of Denmark, which is the state of the nation, the pulse of the world's body, and a manifestation of the spiritual sickness or health of its particular citizens. It is no wonder that Hamlet thinks of himself so consistently both as physician and avenger.

In tragedy the action is developed by intensification. Some difficulty that may have seemed slight at the beginning of a play is intensified by repetition and emphasis, and it is made to seem progressively graver and more destructive. The characters involve themselves inextricably in that web of circumstances that will constitute their doom. Things change in tragedy, usually for the worse, and there is a sense that no one can resist the tragic momentum. The force of evil in tragedy does not permit the kind of complications that dominate comedy, where the audience is expected to admire the dancelike ingenuity of the plot. Instead, the evil in tragedy has metaphysical and religious overtones, and, by the workings of empathy and catharsis, the audience is expected to feel pity and fear for the events on stage. Tragedy is threatening, minatory, and instructive.

Othello best illustrates the structural pattern of a Shakespearean tragedy, because the play is so beautifully articulated within a narrow range. Once Iago begins to work on Othello's emotions, there is a progressive deterioration in the Moor. The effect is indicated stylistically, as Othello picks up Iago's mannerisms: his insinuating repetitions, his broken syntax, his teasing questions, his persistent references to gross animals. In the long third scene of Act III, we move by sure steps to the confirmation of Othello's jealousy. Toward the beginning of the scene, is he still demanding openness from Iago:

> Think, my lord! By heaven, he echoes me,
> As if there were some monster in his thought
> Too hideous to be shown. Thou dost mean
>   something:
> I heard thee say but now thou lik'st not
>   that,
> When Cassio left my wife. What didst not
>   like?
>
> (3.3.110–14)

Gradually, Othello's own lucidity gives way to uncontrollable indignation: "Ha! ha! false to me, to me?" (337). By the end of the scene, he is swearing vengeance like the blackest of stage revengers:

> Damn her, lewd minx! O, damn her, damn
>   her!

Come, go with me apart; I will withdraw
To furnish me with some swift means of
    death
For the fair devil. Now art thou my
    lieutenant.

(3.3.479–82)

We feel vividly the tragic intensification of this scene. Othello is not the same person at the end as he was at the beginning. By his own commitment, he is moving inevitably to his tragic fate. Othello is not just an innocent victim of Iago's cleverness; he is also vulnerable to Iago and irresistibly attracted to him. Perhaps we should speak of the Iago aspect of Othello, which gradually shows itself in Act III, scene iii. This formulation circumvents the simple notion of a change in character. That Othello is utterly misinformed and tricked by Iago is only part of the dramatic irony; the important point is that Othello has given his consent to what is happening to him. He is an active participant in his own tragedy.

In *Macbeth*, we feel the intensification of the tragic action so strongly that the emphasis falls on the middle of the play rather than the end. Macbeth begins with an acute moral sensitivity. His first substantial aside already poses the problem of guilty ambition that preys upon his conscience:

This supernatural soliciting
Cannot be ill; cannot be good. If ill,
Why hath it given me earnest of success,
Commencing in a truth? I am Thane of
    Cawdor.
If good, why do I yield to that suggestion
Whose horrid image doth unfix my hair
And make my seated heart knock at my ribs
Against the use of nature?

(1.3.130–37)

Macbeth is echoing the moral ambiguity of the witches' "Fair is foul, and foul is fair" (1.1.10). The murder of Duncan is an agonizing experience because Macbeth is so vividly aware of what he is doing. He seizes on hallucinatory details to stand self-judged and self-condemned, as in his recollection of Duncan's grooms:

> One cried 'God bless us', and 'Amen' the
>   other,
> As they had seen me with these hangman's
>   hands.
> List'ning their fear, I could not say 'Amen'
> When they did say 'God bless us!'
>   (2.2.26–29)

He has begun to feel already the spiritual aridity that will later torment him.

Macbeth's plotting against Banquo and Fleance is more deliberate and impersonal than the murder of Duncan. There is no longer any conflict over his own motives, but only a frenzied desire to be secure:

>   To be thus is nothing,
> But to be safely thus. Our fears in Banquo
> Stick deep; and in his royalty of nature
> Reigns that which would be fear'd.
>   (3.1.47–50)

The escape of Fleance and the appearance of Banquo's Ghost accuse Macbeth not only of blundering, but also of an ironically useless effort against his preordained destiny. Macbeth's sensitivity to his own evil-doing has coarsened, although he is yet "but young in deed" and "wants hard use" (3.4.143–44). As he confides wearily to his wife,

>   I am in blood
> Stepp'd in so far that, should I wade no
>   more,
> Returning were as tedious as go o'er.
>   (3.4.136–38)

"Tedious" is an extraordinary word in this context, and it clearly marks the end of Macbeth's moral perturbation.

The murder of Macduff's children is an additional outrage, but nothing seems to matter to Macbeth any longer. His physical and moral sensitivity has been dulled:

I have almost forgot the taste of fears.
The time has been my senses would have
   cool'd
To hear a night-shriek, and my fell of hair
Would at a dismal treatise rouse and stir
As life were in't. I have supp'd full with
   horrors;
Direness, familiar to my slaughterous
   thoughts,
Cannot once start me.

$$(5.5.9-15)$$

Apathy and cynicism have replaced Macbeth's hyperactive conscience: "My way of life/ Is fall'n into the sear, the yellow leaf" (5.3.22–23), and life itself is now only "a tale/ Told by an idiot, full of sound and fury,/ Signifying nothing" (5.5.26–28). This represents not so much a change in Macbeth's character as a working-out of issues raised in the opening scenes. There is no possible resolution for Macbeth, so that his end can only be the final step in a chain of circumstances.

Undue importance has been placed on the endings of Shakespeare's tragedies, as if they, more than any other part, could reveal the special meaning of the plays. Critics have justified death in tragedy according to a moral pattern: the protagonist must be punished for his tragic flaw or for whatever character defect precipitated his fall. If the tragic movement brings recognition, the protagonist must pay the price for his newly found awareness; his insight is always dearly bought. Even if we feel a sense of loss and waste, there is still a tacit affirmation that the ways of providence are just, albeit inscrutable.

I find a certain glibness in these formulations, which insist that there is a system of rewards and punishments in Shakespeare that has ceased to function in ordinary experience. Tragedies end in death, but death is mysterious and Shakespeare offers no comforting assurances. In *King Lear*, for example, the deaths show more of outrage than of spiritual reconciliation. True, there is an evolution in the

Gloucester action that is close to the paradigm of tragedy in Aristotle's *Poetics*. Through his blinding, the easy-going, complacent Gloucester comes to new insight about his moral condition:

> I stumbled when I saw: full oft 'tis seen
> Our means secure us, and our mere defects
> Prove our commodities.
>
> (4.1.20–22)

He actually has a double recognition, because, with the help of his son Edgar, he is able to overcome the despair that follows his blinding. After his suicide attempt on Dover Cliffs and the news of King Lear's defeat in battle, Gloucester is willing to assent to the principle of Christian fortitude enunciated by Edgar:

> Men must endure
> Their going hence, even as their coming
>   hither:
> Ripeness is all.
>
> (5.2.9–11)

Gloucester's death exemplifies this beatific wisdom of ripeness. When Edgar reveals his identity, his father's

> flaw'd heart—
> Alack, too weak the conflict to support!—
> 'Twixt two extremes of passion, joy and
>   grief,
> Burst smilingly.
>
> (5.3.196–99)

This is not tragic at all, and there is something painfully artificial in Edgar's moral affirmations: "The gods are just, and of our pleasant vices/ Make instruments to plague us" (5.3.170–71). If this were true, *King Lear* would be a Sunday school exemplum, but Edgar's formula is not true even for Gloucester. To prove that "The gods are just," Edgar cites his brother's bastardy: "The dark and vicious place where thee he got/ Cost him his eyes" (172–73). But how can we reduce the savage scene of the blinding of Gloucester (3.7) to a fitting punishment for his loose morality? This scene is so intensely cruel in all of its physical details just because it has no relation at all to Gloucester's carnal offenses. He is caught by his enemies while attempting to succor Lear, and he is mocked and tormented by Cornwall and Regan in order to intensify the outrage. This is Shakespeare's most direct experiment in the theater of cruelty.

In the main action, it is even more difficult to locate that "dark viciousness" that costs Lear his life. As in all tragedy, there is an overwhelming disproportion between the result and the cause, between the death of the protagonist and the weaknesses in character and errors in judgment that precipitate that death. The comforting theory of the tragic flaw simplifies tragedy, so that everything seems to happen according to rational necessity. What is Lear's tragic flaw? Is it vanity, overweening, petulance, irresponsibility—the vices he demonstrates in the opening scene with his daughters? Once Lear makes the first step to set his tragedy in motion, it proceeds of its own momentum and without any relation at all to his original flaw. The difficulties intensify until Lear's reason cracks, but from his madness on the heath comes a new understanding of things and a new simplicity. This is the fullest and most extended recognition in Shakespeare: "You must bear with me./ Pray you now, forget and forgive; I am old and foolish" (4.7.84–85). Lear's death at the end is not unexpected; like Gloucester and Kent (whose death is imminent), he has outlived his time.

It is Cordelia's death that defines the tragedy of *King Lear*. After her capture, she understands that her tragic fate is linked with her father's:

> We are not the first
> Who with best meaning have incurr'd the worst.
> For thee, oppressed King, am I cast down;
> Myself could else out-frown false Fortune's frown.

> (5.3.3–6)

To incur the worst, even with "best meaning," is radically different from Edgar's pat assertion that "The gods are just." With the wisdom of anticipation, Cordelia knows that she will be a sacrifice for Lear. Why is her death necessary? Surely we cannot believe that her taciturnity in the first scene is an authentic tragic flaw that incites the wrath of the gods. Nahum Tate skirted the problem in his Restoration version by marrying Cordelia off to Edgar. Her death pains us and outrages us as does perhaps no other death in Shakespearean tragedy, because it is so unrelated to any sufficient cause. It is gratuitous and it is cruel. Perhaps that is what the tragic ending is meant to be, rather than an affirmation of moral rightness and justice.

The climax of *Romeo and Juliet* also evokes this sense of outrage, because the deaths of the protagonists cannot properly be attributed to any faults in character. Even their rashness is in response to the importunate demands of the action, however much it may be colored by tragic foreboding. They are a sacrifice to the malevolence of Verona, a city much like Shylock's Venice and Timon's Athens. In this sense, Romeo and Juliet are the tragic scapegoats—lovers in a city of hate—whose blood is needed to clense the communal guilt. Capulet calls them "Poor sacrifices of our enmity" (5.3.303), which is a point the prologue of the play has already made: "And the continuance of their parents' rage,/ Which, but their children's end, nought could remove." Prince Escalus expounds the same notion in the final scene:

> Capulet, Montague,
> See what a scourge is laid upon your hate,
> That heaven finds means to kill your joys
>   with love!
> And I, for winking at your discords too,
> Have lost a brace of kinsmen. All are
>   punish'd.
>
> (5.3.290–94)

So the Capulets and Montagues make their peace, and we are forbidden to ask whether the deaths of Romeo and Juliet can be justified.

An aspect of tragedy related to the tragic ending is the

feeling of pity that is so powerfully aroused just before the catastrophe. By the workings of tragic anticipation, the inevitable end penetrates the middle and even the beginning of the play. Instead of suspense, which may be meretricious, we are permitted to experience the events of the play superimposed upon their outcome. We suffer proleptically for what will occur and must occur even while it is in the process of happening.

In *Othello*, for example, even while the Moor is raging against Desdemona and preparing her death, he suddenly feels a sense of compassion both for himself and for her:

> Ay, let her rot, and perish, and be damn'd
> to-night; for she shall not live. No, my heart
> is turn'd to stone; I strike it, and it hurts my
> hand. O, the world hath not a sweeter crea-
> ture; she might lie by an emperor's side and
> command him tasks.

$$(4.1.177-81)$$

The quick turns of this speech are not subject to character analysis, since Othello suddenly sees himself as he will be at the end of the play, and he feels acutely that hardness of heart of which he will be consciously aware only after he has murdered Desdemona. The gesture of striking his heart and hurting his hand emphasizes his torment. With satanic consistency and single-mindedness, Iago despises Othello's emotions and grudges him any trace of compassion: "Nay, that's not your way" (182). But Othello continues covertly to celebrate Desdemona's attraction until he can see his own tragedy and hers not as a participant, but as an observer: "But yet the pity of it, Iago! O, Iago, the pity of it, Iago!" (191–92). He is appealing for a human sympathy Iago is incapable of rendering, and the repetition defines Othello's agony. "It" is deliberately vague, so that "pity" may be a term for Othello's feelings for Desdemona as well as for the murder he must commit. He also feels pity for himself.

Othello develops this anticipatory pity more fully than any other tragedy of Shakespeare. A whole scene is devoted to Desdemona's going to bed just before she is strangled in that bed by Othello. It is a ritualistic scene, in which Desdemona acts out the role of sacrificial victim. She has Emilia lay her wedding sheets on the bed, and she instructs her: "If I do die before thee, prithee shroud me/ In one of these same sheets" (4.3.23–24). Desdemona then sings her "song of 'willow,'" that she heard from her mother's maid, Barbary, whose love "prov'd mad,/ And did forsake her" (26–27). The anticipations of death are gently and lyrically gathered by Desdemona, who does nothing at all to countermand her imminent doom. The pity she arouses is more prolonged than Othello's but equally intense; both force us to consider the middle of the play in the perspective of the tragic end.

Tragic anticipation controls that quiet moment when the protagonist stops struggling and seems to consent to his doom. This moment generally follows the recognition and precedes the catastrophe, and it represents a new clarity of vision, in which the protagonist can understand what is happening to him in an impersonal, omniscient way. By this means, the inevitable death at the end is not unexpected. Whether it is justified or not—and I think we are committed to believing that it can never be justified in any proportional sense—the protagonist finally is ready to die.

As Hamlet phrases it, "the readiness is all" (5.2.215–16), and his talk with Horatio just before the fencing match defines at its best that paradoxical moment that mixes tragic premonition with spiritual tranquillity. Hamlet believes he will defeat Laertes, but yet, as he tells Horatio, "thou wouldst not think how ill all's here about my heart; but it is no matter" (203–5). It is "such a kind of gain-giving as would perhaps trouble a woman" (207–8). Horatio, who is the epitome of good sense and reasonableness—"A man that Fortune's buffets and rewards/ Hast ta'en with equal thanks" (3.2.65–66)—advises his friend not to fight, but for Hamlet it is impossible to refuse:

> ... we defy augury: there is a special provi-
> dence in the fall of a sparrow. If it be now,

'tis not to come; if it be not to come, it will
be now; if it be not now, yet it will come—
the readiness is all.

$$(5.2.211-15)$$

"It" presumably means death, for which Hamlet is now
ready. Providence, which looks out for the fall of a
sparrow, will certainly also provide for Hamlet's still
mysterious fate. We cannot avoid what "will come."

The World of the Play: Theatrical Significances

What are Shakespeare's plays about?

❪ This is perhaps the most difficult question of all, because there are so many different valid answers that no single answer is satisfactory. And as the answers become fuller, they also begin to include more and more disturbing polarities. It is certainly a much simpler task to say what the plays are not about. We know, for example, that Lily B. Campbell's categories in *Shakespeare's Tragic Heroes: Slaves of Passion* cannot possibly describe the wide range of Shakespearean tragedy. She sees each of the major tragedies as a mirror of a particular passion. It comes as no surprise to learn that jealousy dominates *Othello* and fear *Macbeth*, but is *Hamlet* "A Tragedy of Grief" and *King Lear* "A Tragedy of Wrath in Old Age"? If jealousy, fear, grief, and wrath play a role in all of these plays, they are in no sense what the plays are about. Even the jealousy of Othello, which is the most obvious category, grows out of moral failings that are more significant than the passion itself. Jealousy is only the outward sign of Othello's tragic vulnerability. And King Lear's wrath is hardly the center of his tragedy. When he knows finally, "I am a very foolish fond old man" (4.7.60), there is no sense at all that what he learns through suffering is how to control his temper. This is to reduce the complex and mysterious tragedy of Lear to a self-improvement formula.

One way to explain what a Shakespearean play is about is to consider that play in terms of the imaginative world it creates. This approach avoids simplified conclusions by insisting on both sides of the equation—protagonist and antagonist, main plot and subplot—without attempting to reconcile opposing forces or balance out apparent contradictions. In *Antony and Cleopatra*, for example, it would be wrong to say that the values of Rome triumph over those of Egypt, despite the fact that the protagonists die at the end. It would be just as wrong to see in these deaths the triumph of Egypt and everything it represents. In the world of the play, the tragic conflict cannot ultimately be resolved—that is why it is a tragedy rather than a moral demonstration. Rome doesn't cancel out Egypt, and there is no need to reject one in order to embrace the other. Caesar is in the play as well as Cleopatra, and neither Antony nor Enobarbus knows what course of action to follow. Antony remains in Egypt against his better judgment, and the rational decision of Enobarbus to desert Antony proves to be heart-breakingly wrong. Choices are perilous in tragedy, and the unmanageable paradoxes do not disappear once the tragic resolution has been reached. It seems to me that nothing at all ever disappears in tragedy or comedy; like matter, themes may change form, but they cannot be eliminated.

In *As You Like It*, we may see the analogical patterns in the world of this play with special clarity. The main action is generated by love at first sight. Orlando and Rosalind are magnetically drawn to each other, and although Fortune scatters them, they meet again in the Forest of Arden, where Rosalind is in male disguise as Ganymede, a page. Not recognizing his beloved, Orlando soliloquizes his unrequited passion:

> O Rosalind! these trees shall be my books,
> And in their barks my thoughts I'll
>   character,
> That every eye which in this forest looks
> Shall see thy virtue witness'd every where.
> Run, run, Orlando; carve on every tree,

The fair, the chaste, and unexpressive
[= inexpressible] she.
(3.2.5–10)

Orlando busies himself with his carving, and he also hangs his love poems on the trees. Despite his solitary situation, he seems to have a keen eye for publicity.

Rosalind never reveals her affection so openly. Like all Shakespeare's heroines, she prefers indirect and disguised forms of expression, especially witty ones, and she makes fun of the very romantic love by which she is enthralled. As she tells Orlando in the dialogue where she coyly pretends to be Rosalind:

> The poor world is almost six thousand years old, and in all this time there was not any man died in his own person, videlicet, in a love-cause. Troilus had his brains dash'd out with a Grecian club; yet he did what he could to die before, and he is one of the patterns of love. Leander, he would have liv'd many a fair year, though Hero had turn'd nun, if it had not been for a hot midsummer-night; for, good youth, he went but forth to wash him in the Hellespont, and, being taken with the cramp, was drown'd; and the foolish chroniclers of that age found it was—Hero of Sestos. But these are all lies: men have died from time to time, and worms have eaten them, but not for love.
> (4.1.83–95)

By ridiculing the classical exemplars of love, Rosalind gives her argument a special emphasis, yet this is part of her own amorous badinage with Orlando.

Romantic love is mercilessly burlesqued in the pastoral subplot of Phebe, the "proud disdainful" shepherdess, and Silvius, the helpless, doting shepherd. Silvius has some absurd moments in the play, in which we see him as the slavish dependent of his mistress, bearing her love letters to Ganymede. As he confesses to Phebe:

> So holy and so perfect is my love,
> And I in such a poverty of grace,

That I shall think it a most plenteous crop
To glean the broken ears after the man
That the main harvest reaps; loose now and
   then
A scatt'red smile, and that I'll live upon.
                    (3.5.98–103)

Although Rosalind admits that "The sight of lovers feedeth those in love" (3.4.52), she seems genuinely perturbed by Phebe's aloofness. With Solomonic practicality, she advises the dark and unattractive Phebe to "Sell when you can; you are not for all markets" (3.5.60). The excessively romantic love of Silvius for Phebe (and of Phebe for Ganymede) helps to define one extreme for Rosalind and Orlando.

The other extreme is the sensual wooing of Audrey the goatherdess, "A poor virgin, sir, an ill-favour'd thing, sir, but mine own" (5.4.56–57), by Touchstone the Clown, who is under no illusions about what he is doing: "As the ox hath his bow, sir, the horse his curb, and the falcon her bells, so man hath his desires; and as pigeons bill, so wedlock would be nibbling" (3.3.69–71). The outlandish examples parody the euphuistic style, but Touchstone is erecting a moral framework in order to ridicule moral pretense.

Both Audrey and Phebe set off Rosalind as a mean between extremes, as Orlando is also a mean between Touchstone and Silvius. This represents the character functions in the play too symmetrically, since both Rosalind and Orlando have some qualities of the characters with whom they are contrasted. Neither Rosalind nor Orlando is a fixed, dogmatic entity. On the other hand, to say that Touchstone speaks the witty, unclouded wisdom of Shakespeare is equally untenable. Young love is celebrated in *As You Like It*, as it is in all of Shakespeare's romantic comedies. That is the point of comedy, which affirms the norms of society by making love culminate in marriage. Romantic love is also full of the absurd intensity of Silvius and Phebe, that is mocked by Touchstone and Audrey. But Orlando and Rosalind are not excluded from this youthful absurdity, so that the world of the play must include all three pairs of lovers, each in its own right, and without distorting the natural emphases. No single conclusion is possible about Shakespeare's attitude to romantic love in *As You Like It*; the very sentiments that are most valued are also most freely undercut.

The workings of analogy in Shakespeare are complex. If analogy is an integrating power in the world of the play, it is not also a reductive one, and the integrity of the separate actions and character groups is preserved. One action may be balanced against another, and one character serve as foil for another, but that doesn't mean that the contrasting actions and characters are merely supernumerary. In *A Midsummer Night's Dream*, where there are at least five separate lines of movement, we may admire the articulation with which they are put together into one play. The different voices are counterpointed against each other to create a single composition. Or we may choose to follow the metaphor of the title and endow the separate actions with the free association of dreams. Helena's soliloquy at the end of the first scene indicates the qualities of love that rule the play:

> Things base and vile, holding no quantity,
> Love can transpose to form and dignity.
> Love looks not with the eyes, but with the
> mind;
> And therefore is wing'd Cupid painted blind.
> Nor hath Love's mind of any judgment taste;
> Wings and no eyes figure unheedy haste;
> And therefore is Love said to be a child,
> Because in choice he is so oft beguil'd.
>
> (1.1.232–39)

The truth of Helena's words is confirmed by the mix-ups in the wood near Athens, where love of the most intense sort is chemically induced by Puck.

The assertion that love can transpose "Things base and vile" to "form and dignity" is acted out in Titania's wooing of Bottom the weaver, metamorphosed by the jealous Oberon into an ass. Bottom is wonderfully adapted to his new role, which carries over directly from his acting of

Pyramus. Titania is now his Thisbe, and she is like one of those Greek goddesses who become enamored of a mortal and promise to make him a god:

> And I will purge thy mortal grossness so
> That thou shalt like an airy spirit go.
>
> (3.1.146–47)

But despite all enchantments Bottom remains himself. He handles his new situation with a becoming delicacy of phrase: "I must to the barber's, mounsieur; for methinks I am marvellous hairy about the face; and I am such a tender ass, if my hair do but tickle me I must scratch" (4.1.22–24). Is this episode intended to mock the pretensions of romantic love, or is it rather a proof of love's spiritual power, that "looks not with the eyes, but with the mind"? In the oneiric atmosphere of *A Midsummer Night's Dream* all things are possible.

I am insisting on a proposition so simple that it may be overlooked: everything in a play is part of the world of that play and has its own validity. The villain and the protagonist are related, and one depends upon the other in order to exist. No murderer likes the stain of blood, because that proves to him that he is a murderer and not the priestly sacrificer he hoped to be. Othello strangles Desdemona in her bed because he doesn't want to "shed her blood" (5.2.3), and Brutus thinks of the assassination of Caesar as a holy ritual:

> Let's be sacrificers, but not butchers, Caius.
> We all stand up against the spirit of Caesar,
> And in the spirit of men there is no blood.
> O that we then could come by Caesar's
>   spirit,
> And not dismember Caesar! But, alas,
> Caesar must bleed for it!
>
> (2.1.166–71)

Without realizing it, Brutus is explaining how villains and heroes become part of each other in tragedy. Brutus is implicated in murder against his conscious will, but from Cassius's viewpoint, the innocence of Brutus is indispensable for the conspiracy.

In *Othello*, we can never know whether Iago really hates the Moor, or whether, in some obscure way, he loves him and wishes to take possession of him. Isn't Othello irresistibly attracted to Iago, fascinated by him, so that Iago's discourse has an hypnotic interest unlike that of any other character? We need to explain this relation between Othello and Iago in terms of the world of the play. Whatever his moral status, Iago has extraordinary dramatic attraction. If we pursue this kind of reasoning, we find in Macbeth both Othello and Iago now made into a single character. The villain-hero is Dr. Faustus and Mephostophilis together. Macbeth's tenderness of conscience does not prevent him from murdering King Duncan; it only makes it more difficult for him, as Lady Macbeth understands with such chilling clarity.

Shakespeare is not a philosopher, or a psychologist, or even an original thinker, and we limit our understanding of the plays to consider him as such.

❨ Shakespeare's plays may have a subject, a theme, a context of ideas, and sometimes a lively intellectual debate, but there is a difference between discursive reasoning presented for its own sake and the reasonings of characters within the dramatic action. Even in such "problem" plays as *Measure for Measure, Troilus and Cressida,* and *Hamlet,* where abstract ideas are debated with passionate earnestness, the argument is not what the play is about, but is used rather as a vehicle for presenting characters at moments of crisis, where the intellectual position defines a moral commitment.

Troilus and Cressida sets Greeks and Trojans as much against each other in their discussions of policy as on the battlefield. The argument in the Greek camp begins with Agamemnon's question: Why, "after seven years'

siege yet Troy walls stand" (1.3.12)? The Greek failure
is

> nought else
> But the protractive trials of great Jove
> To find persistive constancy in men ....
> (1.3.19–21)

The latinate antitheses are meant to characterize Agamemnon as a bombastic fool—his ponderous style calls
attention to the emptiness of his moral platitudes. Similarly, the labyrinthine figures of Old Nestor tell us more
about his own tedious senescence than about the flagging
Greek war effort.

It is not until the oration of Ulysses that we begin to
understand what is wrong: "The specialty of rule hath
been neglected" (1.3.78). "Degree," which is the basis
of hierarchical order in man, the state, and the cosmos,
has been "vizarded" (83) and "shak'd" (101). "Take but
degree away, untune that string,/ And hark what discord
follows!" (109–10). Commentators tend to give this
grand speech excessive importance just because it so
eloquently rephrases the commonplaces of the Elizabethan world picture. What is actually undermining
the Greeks is that their chief warrior, Achilles, refuses
to fight, and the wily Ulysses sets about trying to activate
him by appealing to his self-love. In this play particularly
there is a striking difference between the characters' lofty
professions and their sordid motives.

The argument in the Trojan camp is more literally a
debate, in which radically different positions are allowed
to conflict openly with each other. Hector's appeal for
reason, moderation, and good sense makes the return of
Helen a matter of moral principle, but his brother Troilus
ridicules the calculating morality of reason:

> Nay, if we talk of reason,
> Let's shut our gates and sleep. Manhood and
>   honour
> Should have hare hearts, would they but fat
>   their thoughts

With this cramm'd reason. Reason and
  respect
Make livers pale and lustihood deject.
(2.2.46–50)

The romantic bravado of this speech has an ironic relation to Troilus's own withering disillusion with Cressida
later in the action. His chivalric sense of personal honor
cannot remain untainted in the world of the play.

Troilus's attack on reason lays the basis for the debate, which is conducted with a strict formality:

> *Hector.* Brother, she is not worth what she
>   doth cost
>   The keeping.
> *Troilus.*   What's aught but as 'tis valued?
> *Hector.* But value dwells not in particular
>   will:
>   It holds his estimate and dignity
>   As well wherein 'tis precious of itself
>   As in the prizer. 'Tis mad idolatry
>   To make the service greater than the
>   god;
>   And the will dotes that is attributive
>   To what infectiously itself affects,
>   Without some image of th' affected
>   merit.
(2.2.51–60)

Hector's abstractions take no account of the weakness
of the audience, which must try to follow the complex
argument from what it hears. But even if the audience
doesn't understand every logical turn, there is an unmistakable intensity in the speakers.

The debate ends in a surprising, perhaps even shock-
ing, way when Hector abandons his own position and
yields to his brothers' conception of honor:

>   Hector's opinion
> Is this, in way of truth. Yet, ne'er the less,
> My spritely brethren, I propend to you
> In resolution to keep Helen still;

> For 'tis a cause that hath no mean
>   dependence
> Upon our joint and several dignities.
>
> (2.2.188–93)

Hector's "truth" cannot withstand the pressures of family solidarity, and his change of heart offers an excellent example of how Shakespeare subordinates abstract argument to the demands of character. Hector is no personified spokesman for a set of ideas, but, rather, he dominates those ideas by his own intrusive presence.

In *Measure for Measure*, abstract moral questions are also dramatized through character and incident, and the formality of the debate sharpens the intensity of the dramatic conflict. The play begins with a long, didactic speech by the Duke of Vienna: "Of government the properties to unfold ..." (1.1.3), which is an unusual (and potentially disastrous) way to open a comedy. This is hardly exposition in the conventional sense, although it does hint darkly at important political and moral issues. We soon learn that the Duke will retire for a while, and that he has appointed Angelo to rule in his absence. Act I, scene iii, reveals the Duke's purpose. By vigorous enforcement of the law, he hopes to reform Vienna, and he also means to try Angelo's strictness of morality:

> Lord Angelo is precise;
> Stands at a guard with envy; scarce confesses
> That his blood flows, or that his appetite
> Is more to bread than stone. Hence shall we
>   see,
> If power change purpose, what our seemers
>   be.
>
> (1.3.50–54)

"Precise" is a scornful word in Elizabethan usage, meaning punctilious, overscrupulous (especially in matters of conscience), and it was specifically applied to Puritan hypocrisy. Angelo's first judicial decision is to condemn Claudio to death for getting Julietta with child, even though he is betrothed to her by precontract. The action of the play tests the moral principles on which law and

justice are founded: Should one be judged by the Old
Testament rule of "measure for measure," or by the New
Testament law of love, which tempers justice with mercy?
In his rigidity, Angelo is an Old Testament Pharisee,
while Isabella, the sister of Claudio, pleads for Christian
love to mitigate the letter of the law.

The argument is couched in the formal terms of a
debate:

> *Angelo.* Your brother is a forfeit of the law,
>   And you but waste your words.
> *Isabella.*   Alas! alas!
>   Why, all the souls that were were
>   forfeit once;
>   And He that might the vantage best have
>   took
>   Found out the remedy. How would you
>   be
>   If He, which is the top of judgment,
>   should
>   But judge you as you are? O, think on
>   that;
>   And mercy then will breathe within
>   your lips,
>   Like man new made.
>   (2.2.71–79)

It is, of course, an unfair debate, since Angelo makes it
clear that he has the arbitrary power to enforce his reasoning. In his conversation with Escalus, he is the spokesman
for an arid legalism:

> 'Tis one thing to be tempted, Escalus,
> Another thing to fall. I not deny
> The jury, passing on the prisoner's life,
> May in the sworn twelve have a thief or two
> Guiltier than him they try. What's open
>   made to justice,
> That justice seizes. What knows the laws
> That thieves do pass on thieves?
>   (2.1.17–23)

By the workings of dramatic irony, Angelo is con-
demned by his own speeches, but he is saved in the end

by the Duke's mercy, the human equivalent of divine grace. There is also strong irony in the fact that Angelo's argument is made progressively more rational, even rationalized, in order to disguise his overpowering eroticism. This contrast between what the character is saying and what he is thinking has made Angelo's limited role the major acting part in the play. In this histrionic perspective, there are striking similarities between Isabella and Angelo. Both are troubled, if not actually tormented, by the personal implications of their abstract arguments, and both are made to suffer for the unyieldingness of their public professions.

Shakespeare's art is highly self-conscious. He often breaks the dramatic illusion to let us know that this is only a play and the characters only actors.

◖ In our limited survey of what Shakespeare's plays may be about, we should remember that they are also sometimes about themselves. That is, the playwright abandons any attempt at psychological realism and reminds us that he is an author writing a play, which we as audience are watching. It is all a fiction, pretense, make believe, a willing suspension of disbelief which is never allowed to become involuntary. There is a danger that the audience might become too involved in the illusion, and the playwright, as it were, feels the need to call them to their senses.

Prospero the magician is the closest analogue to Shakespeare the dramatist, because he so openly invokes the thaumaturgic powers to aid him in his work. With the help of the unruly, panurgic forces who answer his call, he produces visions and apparitions that are frankly histrionic. At the end of *The Tempest*, the shipwreck of the first scene is shown to be merely an illusion. As the boatswain reports, the "royal, good, and gallant ship," "in all her trim," is now "tight and yare, and bravely rigg'd, as when/ We first put out to sea" (5.1.236–37, 224–25). The ship is not only still intact, but it also seems to be magically freshened from the stains of its long voyage. Prospero is a showman who puts on the masque and anti-masque of the banquet (3.2) as well as the wedding masque for Ferdinand and Miranda. As he explains to his admiring son-in-law, the actors are

> Spirits, which by mine art
> I have from their confines call'd to enact
> My present fancies.
>
> (4.1.120–22)

There is polite self-deprecation in "My present fancies," but Prospero is intent on his performance.

He closes his masque with a gracious lyric speech, full of the spectacular artifice of the theater:

> Our revels now are ended. These our actors,
> As I foretold you, were all spirits, and
> Are melted into air, into thin air;
> And, like the baseless fabric of this vision,
> The cloud-capp'd towers, the gorgeous
>   palaces,
> The solemn temples, the great globe itself,
> Yea, all which it inherit, shall dissolve,
> And, like this insubstantial pageant faded,
> Leave not a rack behind.
>
> (4.1.148–56)

"Cloud-capp'd towers," "gorgeous palaces," and "solemn temples" are all part of the marvelous scenes of masques, and "the great globe itself" may be a scenic machine as well as an allusion to Shakespeare's Globe. This passage beautifully acknowledges that any "pageant" is bound to be "insubstantial," a figment of the writer's imagination and the audience's apprehension. I don't mean to allegorize *The Tempest* and make Prospero the type of the Creative Spirit, but his own awareness of histrionic illusion is like the self-consciousness I am so freely attributing to Shakespeare.

If "All the world's a stage" (*As You Like It* 2.7.139),

as the melancholy Jaques says in a traditional trope, then it follows that "All the stage is a world," because the theater is a microcosm of that larger world that it depicts. In the pageant-wagon staging of the medieval plays in the biblical cycles, not only is the stage the world, but the area beneath the stage is hell and above it heaven. Some of this literal symbolism of the stage levels persists in Shakespeare. The Ghost in *Hamlet* cries "Swear" from *"under the stage"* (1.5.149 s.d.), and its movements there identify it as "truepenny" (150), "old mole" (162), and a "worthy pioneer" (163), or digger. If this is not a devil, Hamlet's words indicate a gnome or earth spirit. In *Macbeth*, too, the witches are closely connected with the area beneath the stage.

From the opposite direction, gods and goddesses descend to the stage from above, especially in the masque effects of Shakespeare's late plays. These spectacular descents are bound to seem more impressive in performance than in reading. To uplift the "low-laid" Posthumus in *Cymbeline* (5.4.103), *"*JUPITER *descends in thunder and lightning, sitting upon an eagle. He throws a thunderbolt"* (92 s.d.). His ascent to his "palace crystalline" (113) is equally spectacular, perhaps more so, because it makes greater demands on the stage machinery. In *The Tempest*, *"*JUNO *descends in her car"* (4.1.74 s.d.), or chariot, to participate in the wedding masque for Ferdinand and Miranda.

The upper stage in the Elizabethan public theater is sometimes used metaphorically to suggest elevation, especially in *Antony and Cleopatra*, when the dying Antony is laboriously lifted up to Cleopatra in her monument: *"They heave Antony aloft to Cleopatra"* (4.15.37 s.d.). Antony dies in an atmosphere of lyric exclamation, in which "this dull world" becomes in his absence "No better than a sty" (61–62), and it is at this point that Cleopatra resolves to follow him "after the high Roman fashion" (87) of suicide.

The celebrated "balcony" scene of *Romeo and Juliet* also gains some quality of symbolic height from the fact that Juliet is *"above at a window"* (2.2.1 s.d.). Romeo first speaks of her as a celestial being, "the sun" (3), far distant from man's admiring gaze, and her eyes are twinkling in the spheres of "Two of the fairest stars in all the heaven" (15). Romeo's rapturous words have a curiously literal reference to the stage situation:

> O, speak again, bright angel, for thou art
> As glorious to this night, being o'er my head,
> As is a winged messenger of heaven
> Unto the white-upturned wond'ring eyes
> Of mortals that fall back to gaze on him,
> When he bestrides the lazy-pacing clouds
> And sails upon the bosom of the air.
> (2.2.26–32)

In theatrical terms, Juliet is indeed o'er Romeo's head, and he himself is gazing at her with "white–upturned wond'ring eyes."

These examples from *Antony and Cleopatra* and *Romeo and Juliet* are exceptional, and the upper stage in Shakespeare does not usually have such strongly symbolic connotations. Most frequently, the upper stage and the tiring-house façade are used to represent the walls of a city. In *King John*, for example, both the English and the French in turn solicit the allegiance of the town of Angiers, whose leading citizens enter *"upon the walls"* (2.1.200 s.d.). But even here, the smug impassivity of the citizens of Angiers is emphasized by their safe position above the combatants. The scornful words of the Bastard call attention to the stage situation:

> By heaven, these scroyles [= scoundrels] of
>   Angiers flout you, kings,
> And stand securely on their battlements
> As in a theatre, whence they gape and point
> At your industrious scenes and acts of death.
> (2.1.373–76)

In *King John*, too, young Prince Arthur enters *"on the walls"* of the castle in which he is imprisoned. As he stands precariously on the upper stage, he debates with himself whether to jump:

> The wall is high, and yet will I leap down.
> Good ground, be pitiful and hurt me
>   not! . . .
> I am afraid; and yet I'll venture it.
> If I get down and do not break my limbs,
> I'll find a thousand shifts to get away.
>
> (4.3.1–2, 5–7)

By the workings of empathy, the audience superimposes what it sees onto the imagined events of the play, and Arthur's fatal leap is extraordinarily convincing. Even if the upper stage is only nine feet from the main acting area, this is still a considerable leap for a boy actor.

Another way of demonstrating Shakespeare's self-conscious art is by the frequent references to acting and the theater in all of his work. The characters play on the distinction between real persons and fictive ones, and we catch ironic glimpses of the actors speaking in their own behalf. In *Twelfth Night*, for example, the plot against Malvolio is so successful that Fabian exclaims with enthusiasm: "If this were play'd upon a stage now, I could condemn it as an improbable fiction" (3.4.121–22). All the acting imagery shares in this doubleness, by which the speaker is both the subject and the object of what he says. In Macbeth's metaphor,

> Life's but a walking shadow, a poor player,
> That struts and frets his hour upon the
>   stage,
> And then is heard no more . . . .
>
> (5.5.24–26)

Macbeth sees himself as this "poor player," and even though he knows that he will be defeated, he maintains his role to the end.

In Shakespeare's plays within plays, we are also forced to contrast the real world of the main play with the artifice of the presented play, which is usually heightened by a formal, archaic style that parodies an outmoded literary type. In *Love's Labour's Lost*, there is a wonderfully naïve self-consciousness about the Show of the Nine Worthies, which is written partly in the old style of rhymed four-

teeners, with a full seven beats to the line. The actors
are amateurs, whom Shakespeare delights to show in difficulties with their parts. The stage fright of Sir Nathaniel,
the curate, in the role of Alexander gives Costard a chance
to intervene as the self-appointed director of the enter-
tainment. He offers himself as the intermediary between
audience and players:

> A conqueror and afeard to speak! Run away
> for shame, Alisander. [*Sir Nath. retires*]
> There, an't shall please you, a foolish mild
> man; an honest man, look you, and soon
> dash'd. He is a marvellous good neighbour,
> faith, and a very good bowler; but for Ali-
> sander—alas! you see how 'tis—a little o'er-
> parted.
>
> (5.2.573–78)

That Sir Nathaniel is "a very good bowler" seems to
atone for his histrionic failings, since acting is, after all,
not such an important skill. Shakespeare's gracious self-
deprecation helps to account for the collapse of other
illusions in the play, and Sir Nathaniel is not the only
one who is "a little o'erparted."

Except for the Induction, *The Taming of the Shrew* is
actually a play within a play, which begins with a rollick-
ing scene: Christopher Sly the tinker is ejected from an
ale-house by Marian Hacket, the fat alewife of Wincot,
for refusing to pay for the glasses he has broken. Like
some lucky quiz contestant, Sly becomes the happy victim of a practical joke, in which he is transported in his
drunken stupor and transformed into a great lord. The
deception is accomplished with a close attention to theatrical details, including Barthol'mew the page to play
the role of the wife, who "will well usurp the grace,/
Voice, gait, and action, of a gentlewoman" (Induction,
Scene i, 129–30). A troupe of players is conveniently at
hand, which will entertain Sly with a performance of
The Taming of the Shrew. Sly and his Lady are "*aloft*,"
on the upper stage, while the play is being presented below on the main stage. Thus, the double point of view is

established visually for the audience, but Shakespeare doesn't make much effort to sustain it beyond the Induction.

There is a certain similarity between the traveling actors in *The Taming of the Shrew* and those in *Hamlet*, who, by their "cunning," are able to execute "some sport in hand" (Induction, Scene i, 89) in both plays. *The Murder of Gonzago, or The Mousetrap* is designed to "catch the conscience of the King" (*Hamlet* 2.2.601) through the powerful effects of histrionic persuasion. It is a tribute to Shakespeare's self-conscious belief in his own art that he should make the turning-point of *Hamlet* occur in a play. Like Costard in *Love's Labour's Lost*, Hamlet assumes the role of presenter, so that he may have license to comment freely on the action. He taunts Claudius with the ironic resemblances between play world and real world: "'Tis a knavish piece of work; but what of that? Your Majesty, and we that have free souls, it touches us not. Let the galled jade wince, our withers are unwrung" (3.2.235–37). And he gives Claudius his sardonic assurance that it is all only a crude, old play: "they do but jest, poison in jest; no offense i' th' world" (229–30). The Player King is enacting Claudius's murder of Hamlet's father, but who is the Player King and who is the real king? By laying bare the origins of Claudius's power, Hamlet makes him seem merely a king "in jest."

Shakespeare's characters are constantly asserting themselves on different planes of awareness: they are persons in a play; they might also have roles in a play within the play; and they are always assiduously hinting that they are only actors taking part in theatrical make-believe. As spectators of the play, we are expected to follow these histrionic patterns and to distinguish between different degrees of pretense and reality. It seems to me that Shakespeare makes no attempt at all to persuade us that what we see on stage is actually happening in the space and time of ordinary life. As I have been insisting throughout this book, what we admire in Shakespeare is not so much his ability to give us a convincing picture of everyday reality, but rather his skill in making us believe in the reality of his art. We suddenly become aware that "Some squeaking Cleopatra" (5.2.219) played by a boy and the magnificent Cleopatra "O'erpicturing that Venus where we see/ The fancy out-work nature" (2.2.204–5) are one and the same person.

Conclusion

*Shakespeare's resourcefulness,
versatility, and cunning.*

❡ I have been assuming throughout this book that Shakespeare is accessible to intelligent readers and spectators without any special training. We must remember that Shakespeare wrote his plays for a popular audience. Although they have a complexity of design and expression that repays careful study, the plays are not learned in any true sense of the word. I don't agree with the common feeling that only by knowing a great deal about Shakespeare's background can we possibly qualify as readers of his works. It is exhilarating to put oneself into the Elizabethan world picture, or even into the more homely aspects of Elizabethan life and thought. But social and intellectual history is not the same thing as literature, and the background should never become a barrier to the direct experience of the works.

Shakespeare's dramatic conceptions can be immediately understood without any historical knowledge, and audiences radically different from those for whom the plays were written still find them lively, contemporary, and vital. This is the great mystery that critics have been trying to explain. Perhaps one answer is that Shakespeare is constantly changing, developing, and growing to fit the needs and preoccupations of different periods. There is no single, immutable Shakespeare written down once and for all in the early seventeenth century. Shakespeare's plays are our plays, and we are constantly finding significances in them that were never imagined in their own time. As Hamlet tells Horatio in another connection: "There are more things in heaven and earth, Horatio,/ Than are dreamt of in your philosophy."

Our author has wisely maintained his own artistic impersonality above and beyond his works. There is no fatherly or brotherly or avuncular Shakespeare hovering over his actors (as there is a distinct Ben Jonson for all of these roles), and our only guide to the quality of his imagination is the plays themselves. One characteristic that emerges most strongly about Shakespeare is his experimental turn of mind. Once he began a project, he continued it with enthusiasm and a sense of commitment, but when the play was finished, he never returned to the same sort of play again, no matter how successful. In Renaissance terms, he shows remarkable "invention," which is the ability to find something to say in its appropriate form—what we would call imaginative fecundity or creative genius. Shakespeare is constantly trying out different kinds of plays—beginning at the beginning again, as it were—when he could have comfortably remained in his own area of proven competence. He makes a special point of not repeating himself, and even his failures or partial failures are interesting and vital, and his work as a whole shows a notable capacity for growth. Like Picasso, Shakespeare flourishes in an astonishing variety of styles and media. He seems to be as much concerned with pleasing himself as his audience, and he offers an excellent example of what it means to be lively in the arts.

Further Reading

To complete the practical purpose of this book, I would like to suggest some sources of information and interpretation that will help a reader broaden his understanding of Shakespeare. The best place to begin is with a well-annotated edition, which should clarify the main lines of thinking about a particular play. The Signet series (under the general editorship of Sylvan Barnet) is informative and carefully prepared, as is also the Pelican (under the direction of Alfred Harbage), although this edition has a smaller bulk of notes and commentary. The Pelican plays have recently been collected into a single volume, and the collected Signet plays should appear soon. Another useful paperback series, in preparation, is the New Penguin (general editor: T. J. B. Spencer), which is published in England. The most scholarly and authoritative edition of Shakespeare is the Arden (general editors: Harold F. Brooks and Harold Jenkins), now nearing completion. The new Bobbs-Merrill series (general editor: Ian Watt), of which about half a dozen volumes have been published, is similar in scope to the Arden, but with closer attention to the needs of students. An edition interesting for its copious notes, especially about the meanings of words, is that of George Lyman Kittredge, who annotated sixteen plays. This edition has been completed, brought up to date, and abridged by Irving Ribner, and it has just appeared in a single volume. The most idiosyncratic of modern editions is the New Cambridge, under the guidance of John Dover Wilson, whose notes are full of original insights.

Of collected works of Shakespeare by a single editor, the one most often cited by scholars is the Tudor edition by Peter Alexander. It has no notes, but it represents a fresh consideration of the quarto and folio versions that lie behind

a modernized text. Readers of Shakespeare will find it re-
warding to look at some of these original versions as they
first appeared in Shakespeare's lifetime or shortly thereafter.
There is a splended new facsimile of the Shakespeare Folio
of 1623 (edited by Charlton Hinman), and most of the
quartos have been published by Oxford University Press.
These unedited texts are much easier to read than we have
been led to believe, and it is a distinct pleasure to see a
familiar play in Elizabethan spelling, punctuation, and format.

Students of Shakespeare's language can learn a good deal
from the unabridged *Oxford English Dictionary* based on
historical principles (also called the *New English Dictionary*).
The Shakespearean words from the *OED* have been sepa-
rately collected and defined by C. T. Onions in *A Shakespeare Glossary*, which is a handy reference book to sup-
plement the notes in most editions. The old *Shakespeare-
Lexicon* by Alexander Schmidt (revised by Gregor Sarrazin)
is also helpful for its elaborate discrimination of meanings.
Eric Partridge's book, *Shakespeare's Bawdy*, is enlightening
on a special topic.

For readers interested in tracing a certain word or image
through all of Shakespeare's works, John Bartlett's con-
cordance offers a fascinating, analytic guide to the variety of
Shakespeare's imagination. More exhaustive concordances,
produced by computer, are now being published by Marvin
Spevack and T. H. Howard-Hill.

There is an annual listing of books and articles on Shakespeare in *Shakespeare Quarterly, Studies in Philology, Pub-
lications of the Modern Language Association*, and *Shakespeare Survey* (in discussion form). The best general introduction to the vast bibliography of Shakespeare is Ronald
Berman, *A Reader's Guide to Shakespeare's Plays*, which
proceeds play by play and does not hesitate to make strong
personal judgments.

Of general handbooks on Shakespeare, the most authoritative is E. K. Chambers, *William Shakespeare: A Study of
Facts and Problems*. G. E. Bentley's briefer study, *Shakespeare: A Biographical Handbook*, is more recent and makes
an excellent introduction to the known facts of Shakespeare's
career. Many interesting documents about Shakespeare's
Stratford connections are included in Edgar I. Fripp, *Shakespeare: Man and Artist*. A fictionalized but very accurate
account of Shakespeare's life is presented in Marchette

Chute's biography, *Shakespeare of London*, and the history of Shakespearean biography is wittily and exhaustively treated in S. Schoenbaum, *Shakespeare's Lives*.

The Elizabethan background of Shakespeare's plays, especially the background of ideas, has been fully explored in a number of books. The most elementary (and perhaps also the most appealingly coherent) is E. M. W. Tillyard, *The Elizabethan World Picture*. Hardin Craig, *The Enchanted Glass*, and Theodore Spencer, *Shakespeare and the Nature of Man*, offer a fuller exposition. Virgil K. Whitaker addresses himself specifically to *Shakespeare's Use of Learning*. Elizabethan social history is pleasantly chronicled (with photographs) in the two volumes of *Shakespeare's England*.

For Shakespeare's sources, most editions contain brief extracts, but the topic is developed in detail by Geoffrey Bullough in his *Narrative and Dramatic Sources of Shakespeare*, of which six volumes have been published. Bullough's extensive reprints allow us to arrive at our own judgments about Shakespeare's indebtedness, both direct and indirect, to other authors.

In order to understand the kind of theater (or theaters) in which Shakespeare's plays were originally presented, the reader should consult C. Walter Hodges, *The Globe Restored* (second edition), which has many illustrations. A. M. Nagler, *Shakespeare's Stage*, presents a briefer and more introductory account. John Cranford Adams, *The Globe Playhouse* (second edition), should be read with caution, since its conclusions have been seriously questioned by theatrical historians. Bernard Beckerman's book, *Shakespeare at the Globe, 1599–1609*, is especially good for its discussion of dramaturgy.

There are so many critical introductions to Shakespeare that I will mention only three, each of which has a strongly developed point of view. Mark Van Doren's *Shakespeare* and D. A. Traversi's *An Approach to Shakespeare* (third edition) both stress poetic values, especially in the language, whereas Harley Granville-Barker's *Prefaces* puts particular emphasis on acting, staging, and the theater. Roland Frye's recent handbook, *Shakespeare: The Art of the Dramatist*, provides an excellent, comprehensive account.

For further reading on the symbolic approach to Shakespeare, which has figured importantly in the present book, the following are recommended: Caroline Spurgeon, *Shake-*

speare's *Imagery and What It Tells Us*; Wolfgang Clemen, *The Development of Shakespeare's Imagery*; and G. Wilson Knight, *The Wheel of Fire*, *The Imperial Theme*, and other studies. Robert Heilman has written two books on the symbolism of specific plays (*This Great Stage* on *King Lear* and *Magic in the Web* on *Othello*), and Maurice Charney has explored the concept of dramatic imagery in *Shakespeare's Roman Plays* and *Style in "Hamlet."*

About the Author

Born in 1929, Maurice Charney graduated magna cum laude from Harvard College in 1949. He received both his master's degree and his doctorate at Princeton, and he is now a professor of English at Rutgers University.

Mr. Charney is the author of two previous books on Shakespeare, *Style in "Hamlet"* and *Shakespeare's Roman Plays*. He is also the editor of several editions of Shakespeare's plays, among them the Bobbs-Merrill edition of *Julius Caesar* and the Signet edition of *Timon of Athens*.